"THE FOUR SEASONS
AND OTHER VIOLIN CONCERTOS
in Full Score

OPUS 8, COMPLETE

ANTONIO VIVALDI

Edited by Eleanor Selfridge-Field

DOVER PUBLICATIONS, INC.
NEW YORK

ACKNOWLEDGMENTS

The Center for Computer Assisted Research in the Humanities played a very important role in the preparation and production of this edition, which is typeset using its own software system. Frances Bennion and Edmund Correia Jr. deserve much of the credit for finding and correcting small defects in the 1725 print, which forms part of the Center's Vivaldi Database, and Ed deserves all of the credit for the handsome appearance of the music. Enquiries concerning performing materials may be addressed to the Center at 525 Middlefield Road, Suite 120, Menlo Park, CA 94025-3443; tel. (800) JSB-MUSE.

For permission to consult its holdings we gratefully acknowledge the cooperation of the Sächsische Landesbibliothek, Dresden, Germany; the Biblioteca Nazionale Universitaria, Turin, Italy; and the Henry Watson Music Library, Manchester, United Kingdom.

Bibliographical Note

"The Four Seasons" and Other Violin Concertos in Full Score: Opus 8, Complete is a new work, first published by Dover Publications, Inc., in 1995. The publisher is indebted to Dr. Eleanor Selfridge-Field and the Center for Computer Assisted Research in the Humanities, Menlo Park, California, for making this edition possible.

Library of Congress Cataloging-in-Publication Data

Vivaldi, Antonio, 1678–1741.
   [Cimento dell'armonia e dell'inventione]
   "The four seasons" and other violin concertos : in full score, opus 8, complete / Antonio Vivaldi ; edited by Eleanor Selfridge-Field.
   1 score.
   Includes bibliographical references.
   ISBN 0-486-28638-X (pbk.)
   1. Concertos (Violin with string orchestra)—Scores. I. Selfridge-Field, Eleanor.
M1112.V59 op. 8 1995   95-18109
                                                      CIP
                                                        M

Manufactured in the United States of America
Dover Publications, Inc., 31 East 2nd Street, Mineola, N.Y. 11501

CONTENTS

Il Cimento dell'armonia e dell'inventione (The Contest of Harmony and Invention)

Twelve Concertos for Violin, Strings and Continuo
(Opus 8 / early 1720s)

INTRODUCTION

Vivaldi's violin concertos "The Four Seasons" constitute one of the best known and best loved collections of string repertory in our time. Their programmatic nature makes them easily accessible to a general audience. The bird calls in "Spring," the swarms of wasps in "Summer," the hunters' horns in "Autumn," or the narrator's chattering teeth in "Winter" are readily discernible. That these images are so easily communicated by sound alone is, in our visually oriented age, a consoling testimony to the evocative power of aural art.

Less well known are the eight concertos that together with "The Seasons" made up Op. 8. The full collection, *Il Cimento dell'armonia e dell'inventione* ("The Contest of Harmony and Invention"), was issued by the publisher Michel-Charles Le Cène in Amsterdam in 1725. It was dedicated by Vivaldi to the Bohemian Count Wenceslas, Count of Morzin, an advisor to the Austrian Emperor Charles VI.

Vivaldi was engaged as a string teacher in the Venetian Ospedale (orphanage-conservatory) of the Pietà in 1703. Although his first published opus (1705) contained chamber sonatas, Vivaldi soon became involved in the composition of string works—both sonatas and concertos—better suited to the needs of a sacred institution. His reputation as a virtuoso spread rapidly. It attracted daughters of the nobility to seek places in the Pietà's music program, which had originally been designed for foundling girls, and it created great demand abroad for Vivaldi's compositions.

Vivaldi's skills as a composer were enhanced by other callings. In 1713, when his superior Francesco Gasparini moved to Rome, Vivaldi was called upon to compose sacred vocal music for the Pietà. In the same year he became active as a composer of operas. Vivaldi left Venice to direct music for Prince Philip of Hesse-Darmstadt at his court in Mantua at the start of 1718 and stayed for three years.

Vivaldi's theatrical activities had more to do with his instrumental music than might be supposed. His violin solos at intermissions became legendary. According to the account of a German nobleman, J. Fr. A. von Uffenbach, who in 1715 attended three performances of one of Vivaldi's operas, the composer "made his fingers jump to the point where there was only a hair's breadth between them and the bridge. He did this while playing imitative passages on all four strings at incredible speed." In 1724 Vivaldi went to Rome for the production of his opera *Giustino*, which offered a proving ground for the opening theme of "Spring." A simpler version of this theme was used in the sinfonia of Act I. It accompanied the descent of the goddess

Fortuna, on her wheel, to the stage.

Vivaldi explained his reasons for publishing these works in the following way in his dedication of Op. 8:

> Thinking to myself about the long course of years in which I have had the honor of serving Your Highness in the capacity of Master of Music in Italy, I am embarrassed to realize that I have never offered a token of the profound veneration in which I hold you. In consequence I have resolved to print the present volume as a token of my humility at your feet. If among these few, weak concertos you find "The Four Seasons," for so long regarded with indulgence [*compatite*] by the Generous Goodness of Your Highness, I entreat you not to marvel [at my folly], but [rather] to believe that I have thought them worthy of publication because, in fact, they are more substantial [than those you know] insofar as they are accompanied by their sonnets, which contain an absolutely clear declaration of all the things which are depicted in these works. This, I believe, gives them the status of new works . . . . The intelligence that Your Highness possesses in music and the valor of your most virtuous orchestra enable me always to feel confident that my impoverished deeds, in your esteemed hands, will enjoy a greater ascendancy than they merit . . . .

This commentary (the obsequious tone is characteristic of dedications to noble patrons) is unusually informative. It tells us that the works had indeed been circulated, but without their "demonstrative" sonnets, for a number of years. It is evident, both from the commentary and from the music, that they had been polished over a substantial period of time.

The idea of cycles, both natural and man-made, was in vogue at the time among painters, poets, sculptors and philosophers. Bach's *Well-Tempered Clavier*, illustrating the cycle of tonalities, appeared just three years before the publication of Vivaldi's Op. 8. Earlier musical treatments of the seasons included Lully's ballet *Les Saisons* (1661) and an operetta, *Die Vier Jahrszeiten* ("The Four Seasons"), given in Dresden in August 1719 for the wedding of Friedrich August II to Maria Josepha.

Vivaldi does not say who wrote the sonnets on which his works were based. Their texts, which are printed with new translations on pp. x and xi of this edition, are presented in tables that serve three purposes. They show the letter designations that Vivaldi used in linking each section of poetry with the music. They show the divergent rhyme schemes employed. Finally, they show how the segmentation of each sonnet into three musical movements was different.

Far less perfected are the remaining works of Op. 8. Among them there are two further works with naturalistic subtitles—"The Storm at Sea" (No. 5) and "The Hunt" (No. 10)—and one with the more general subtitle "Pleasure" (No. 6), but no specific scripts are provided for these works. In Nos. 5 and 10 it is easy to detect the bobbing boat and the horns of the hunt, but if these works were intended to narrate a sequence of events, that sequence is impenetrable without a text. "Pleasure" is a work of blissful simplicity to which it is difficult to impute any graphic image.

While there are significant differences in style and occasionally some poorly planned transitions in the last eight works, the overall quality of both virtuosic display in fast movements and thoughtful reflection in slow ones is characteristic of Vivaldi's best instrumental works. There is some cohesion in terms of instrumental treatment between concertos 5 through 8 and 9 through 12. It appears that all of the works were composed in the early 1720s.

In relation to the popularity of "The Four Seasons," the scarcity of editions reflecting scholarly discoveries of recent years is surprising. The important work of cataloguing manuscript sources of Vivaldi's music, begun in the 1960s and continuing to the present day by Peter Ryom (RV stands for *Ryom Verzeichnis*), has brought to light handwritten examples for all but two of the concertos—Nos. 6 and 12—in Op. 8. However, for only six of the works (5, 7-11) are there manuscript sources predating the print.

The Turin manuscripts (for 8-11) consist of autograph scores and demonstrate how Le Cène (or an unknown intermediary) revised the works for a larger and perhaps less skilled market. The Dresden materials (Nos. 5, 7, 10) include partial scores made by Vivaldi's Saxon pupil Pisendel and parts that were obviously made later. These demonstrate differences in performance practice between Dresden and Venice. There are also manuscript parts for Nos. 1-5 in Manchester, England; these appear to have been made in Rome in *c*.1740 from the Le Cène print and demonstrate differences between Roman and Venetian performance practice.

Collectively the manuscript sources demonstrate that Vivaldi was quick to change his mind, especially about the solo passages in his concertos. There are numerous discrepancies—especially in Nos. 7, 9 and 11—that have warranted the inclusion of variant readings of such passages from unpublished sources. Numerous small differences in accompaniment style, continuo figuration and bowing are found from source to source.

This new edition, while being based mainly on the 1725 print, gives Vivaldi's (or Pisendel's) bowings and figurations, where available, in the *Violino Principale*. It restores continuo figuration changed in the print to what is found in autograph sources and adds numerous figures to enable today's performers to provide a satisfactory realization. It offers needed corrections to pitches and rhythms. It supplies dynamics markings and ornament indications given erratically in the print. Lastly, it retrieves from Vivaldi's autographs variant readings not available in other editions.

"The Four Seasons": Sonnet Texts

1. *La Primavera* ("Spring")

Mvt.	Sec.	Rhyme	Italian text	English translation
I	A	a	Giunt' è la primavera e festosetti	Spring has come, and birds greet it
	B	b	La salutan gl'augei con lieto canto;	Festively with a cheerful song;
	C	a	E i fonti allo spirar de' zeffiretti	And with the breath of gentle breezes
		b	Con dolce mormorio scorrono intanto.	Springs trickle with a sweet murmur.
	D	b	Vengon' coprendo l'aer di nero amanto,	Lightning and thunder, elected to announce it,
		a	E lampi e tuoni ad annuntiarla eletti.	Come and cover the air with a black cloak.
	E	a	Indi tacendo questi, gl'augelletti	Once they are quiet, the birds
		b	Tornan' di nuovo al lor canoro incanto.	Return to their enchanting song.
II	F	c	E quindi sul fiorito ameno prato	Then on the pleasant, flowered meadow
		d	Al caro mormorio di fronde e piante,	A goatherd, with his faithful dog at his side,
		c	Dorme 'l caprar col fido can' al lato.	Sleeps to the sweet murmur of fronds and plants.
III	G	d	Di pastoral zampogna al suon festante	To the festive sound of a rustic bagpipe
		c	Danzan' ninfe e pastori nel tetto amato	Nymphs and shepherds dance under the beloved canopy
		d	Di primavera all'apparir brillante.	At the brilliant appearance of spring.

2. *L'Estate* ("Summer")

I	A	a	Sotto dura staggion' dal sole accesa	Under the harsh season ignited by the sun
	B	b	Langue l'huom, langue 'l gregge, ed arde il pino;	Man and flock languish, and the pine burns;
		a	Scioglie il cucco la voce, e tosto intesa	The cuckoo offers his voice, and, soon heard,
	C	b	Canta la tortorella e 'l gardelino.	The young turtledove and goldfinch sing.
	D	a	Zeffiro dolce spira, ma contesa	Zephyr[1] blows gently, but suddenly
		b	Muove Borea improviso al suo vicino;	Boreas[2] offers opposition to his neighbor;
	E	a	E piange il pastorel, perche sospesa	And the shepherd weeps, because he fears
		b	Teme fiera borasca, e 'l suo destino.	A severe storm in the offing—and his destiny.
II	F	c	Toglie alle membra lasse il suo riposo	The repose of his tired limbs is disturbed
		d	Il timore de' lampi, e tuoni fieri,	By the fear of lightning and fiery thunder,
		c	E de mosche e mossoni il stuol furioso!	And by a furious swarm of flies and wasps.
III	G	d	Ah, che pur troppo i suoi timor ' son veri.	Unfortunately, his fears are justified.
		c	Tuona e fulmina il Ciel, e grandinoso	The sky thunders and fulminates, and hail
		d	Tronca il capo alle spiche e a' grani alteri.	Flattens ears of corn and majestic grains.

[1] The West Wind.

[2] The North Wind.

3. *L'Autunno* ("Autumn")

Mvt.	Sec.	Rhyme	Italian text	English translation
I	A	a	Celebra il vilanel con balli e canti	The peasant celebrates the blissful pleasure
		b	Del felice raccolto il bel piacere,	Of a happy harvest with dances and songs,
	B	a	E del liquor di Bacco accesi tanti	And, glowing with the liquor of Bacchus,
	C	b	Finiscono col sonno il lor godere.	Many complete their enjoyment with sleep.
II	D	a	Fa ch'ogn'uno tralasci e balli e canti,	The air, tempered by pleasure, makes
		b	L'aria che temperata dà piacere.	Everyone give up dances and songs.
		a	È la staggion ch'invita tanti e tanti	It is the season that invites so many
		b	D'un dolcissimo sonno al bel godere.	To the great enjoyment of a sweet sleep.
III	E	c	I cacciator' alla nov'alba a caccia	At dawn the hunters are off to the hunt
		d	Con corni, schioppi, e canni escono fuore.	With horns, rifles, and dogs.
	F	c	Fugge la belva, e seguono la traccia.	The wild beast flees, and they follow its trail.
	G	d	Già sbigottita, e lassa al gran rumore	Frightened already, and fatigued by the noise
		c	De' schioppi e canni, ferita, minaccia	Of rifles and dogs, wounded, it threatens
	H	d	Languida di fuggir, ma oppressa, muore.	Languidly to flee, but, overcome, it dies.

4. *L'Inverno* ("Winter")

I	A	a	Aggiacciato tremar tra nevi algenti	To tremble from cold in the icy snow,
	B	b	Al severo spirar d'orrido vento,	In the harsh breath of a horrid wind;
	C	b	Correr battendo i piedi ogni momento;	To run, stamping our feet every moment,
	D	a	E pel soverchio gel batter i denti;	Our teeth chattering in the extreme cold.
II	E	a	Passar al fuoco i dì quieti e contenti	Before the fire to pass peaceful,
		b	Mentre la pioggia fuor bagna ben cento.	Contented days while the rain outside pours down.
III	F	b	Caminar sopra 'l giaccio, e a passo lento,	To walk on the ice and, at a slow pace
	G	a	Per timor di cader, girsene intenti.	(For fear of falling), move carefully.
	H	c	Gir[3] forte, sdruzziolar, cader a terra,	To make a bold turn, slip, fall down.
	I	d	Di nuovo ir sopra 'l giaccio e correr forte	To go on the ice once more and run hard
	L	c	Sinch' il giaccio si rompe e si disserra;	Until the ice cracks and breaks up.
	M	d	Sentir uscir dalle ferrate porte	To hear the Sirocco, Boreas, and all
	N	c	Sirocco, Borea, e tutti i venti in guerra.	The winds at war leave their iron gates:
		d	Quest'è 'l verno, ma tal che gioia apporte.	This is winter, but, even so, what joy it brings!

---

[3] "Andare," which does not fit the poetic meter, is found in some partbooks.

BIBLIOGRAPHY

Everett, Paul J. *The Manchester Concerto Partbooks.* 2 vols. New York and London: Garland Publishing, Inc., 1989.

Heller, Karl. *Die deutsche Überlieferung der Instrumentalwerke Vivaldis* (Beiträge zur musik-wissenschaftlichen Forschung in der DDR, 2). Leipzig: VEB Deutscher Verlag für Musik, 1971.

Ryom, Peter. *Les Manuscrits de Vivaldi.* Copenhagen: Antonio Vivaldi Archives, 1977.

Ryom, Peter. *Répertoire des Oeuvres d'Antonio Vivaldi: Les Compositions instrumentales.* Copenhagen: Engstrøm & Sødring AS, 1986.

Selfridge-Field, Eleanor. *Venetian Instrumental Music from Gabrieli to Vivaldi.* 3rd, rev. edn. New York: Dover Publications, Inc., 1994.

Talbot, Michael. *Vivaldi,* rev. edn. London: Dent, 1993.

Vivaldi, Antonio. *Giustino,* ed. Reinhard Strohm. Milan: Ricordi, 1991.

Vivaldi, Antonio. *Il Cimento dell'armonia e dell'inventione: Concerti a 4 e 5, Op. 8.* Facs. edn. New York: Performers' Facsimiles, n.d.

"The Four Seasons"
And Other Violin Concertos

Concerto No. 1 in E Major
La Primavera ("Spring")

I.

Allegro   (A) *Giunt' è la primavera*   (Op. 8, No. 1 / RV 269)

Il canto degl'uccelli [The song of the birds]

1

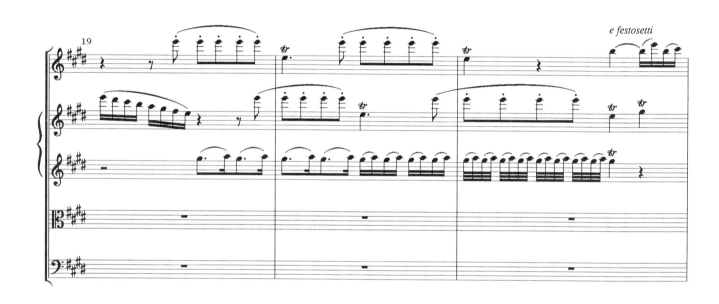

(B) *La salutan gl'augei con lieto canto;*

[Trickling of the springs]
Scorrono i fonti
(C) *E i fonti allo spirar de' zeffiretti   Con dolce mormorio scorrono intanto.*

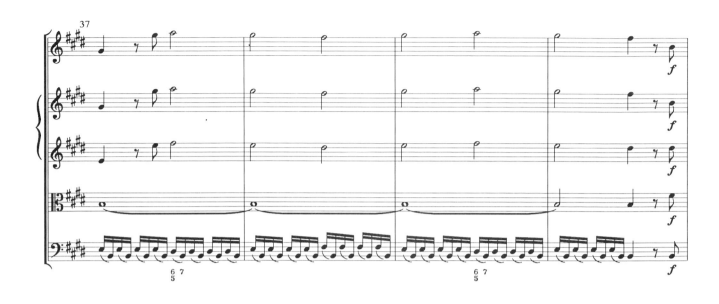

[Thunder]
Tuoni
(D) *Vengon' coprendo l'aer di nero amanto, E lampi e tuoni ad*

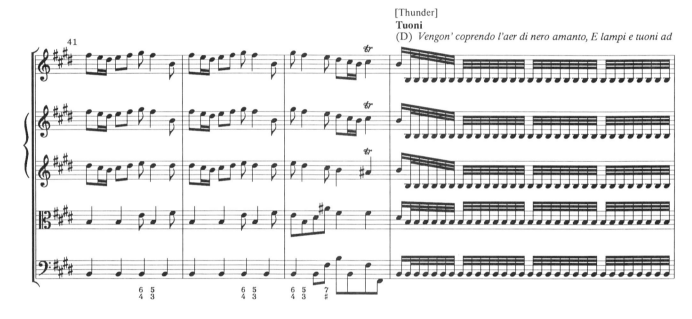

annuntiarla eletti.

[Song of the birds]
Canto degl'uccelli
(E) *Indi tacendo questi, gl'augelletti*   *Tornan' di nuovo al lor canoro incanto.*

Tasto solo

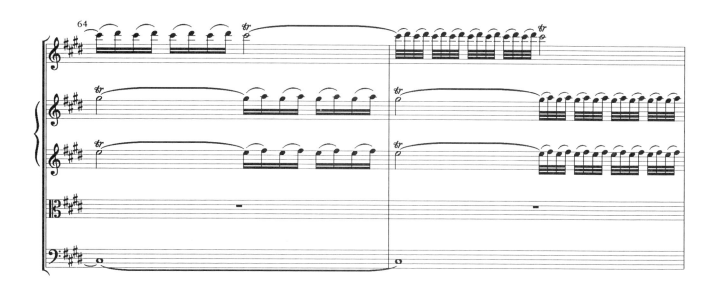

7

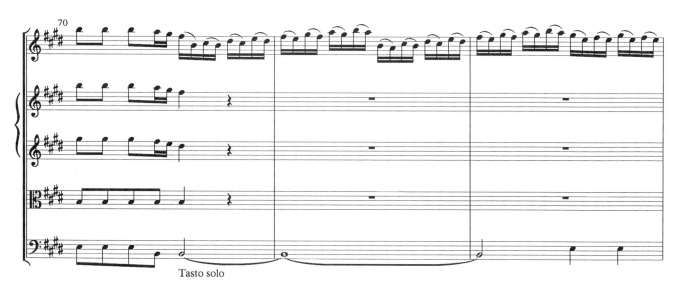

Tasto solo

II.

III.

Tasto solo

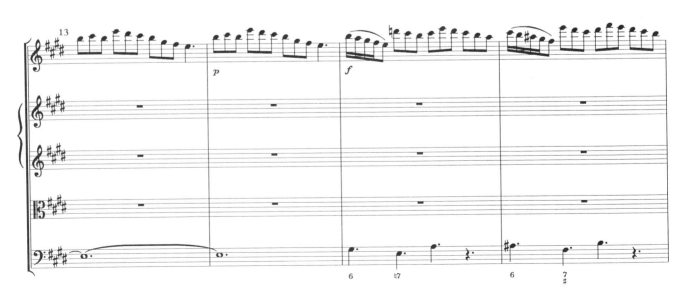

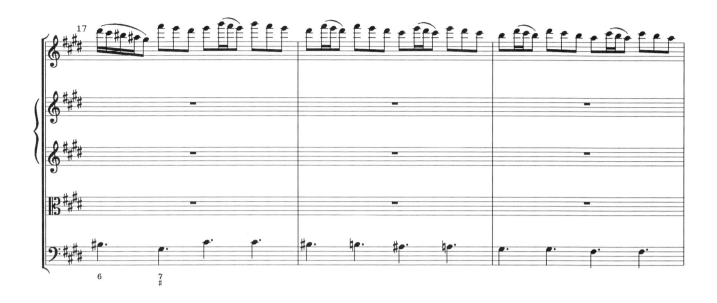

Tasto solo

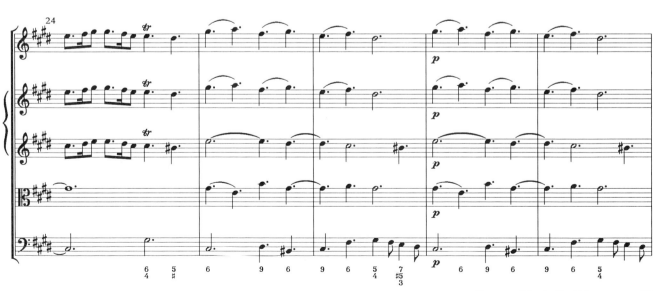

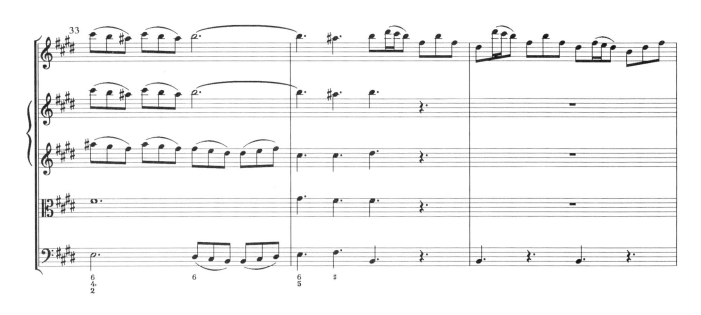

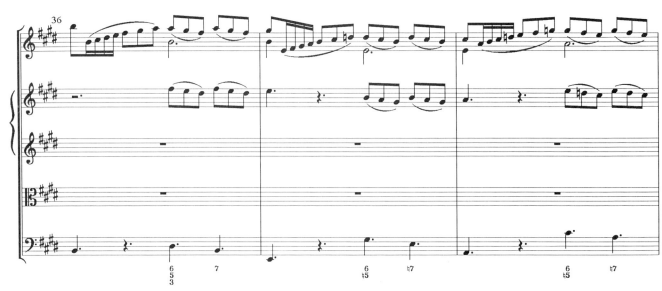

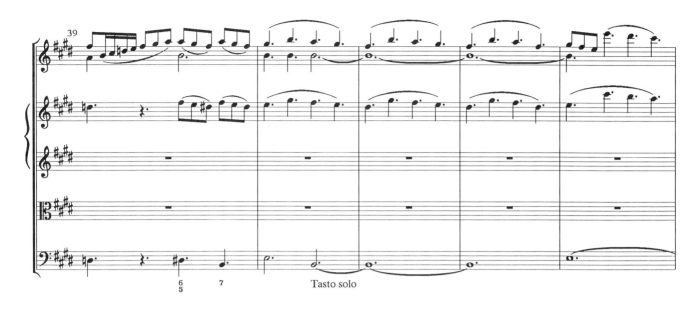

Tasto solo

6
5

7

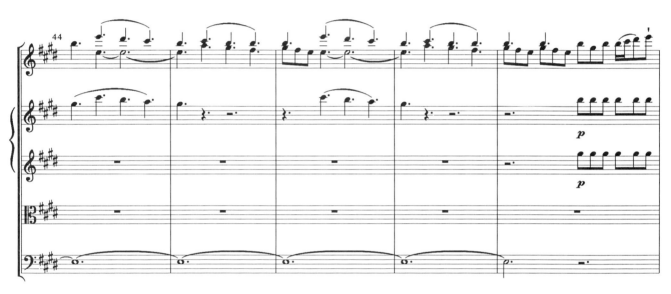

p

p

Tasto solo

16   Concerto No. 1: *La Primavera*

Tasto solo

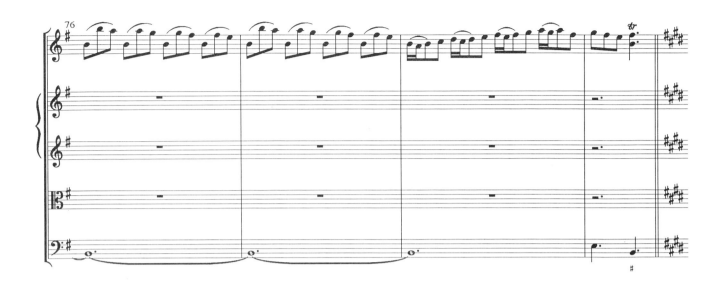

Tasto solo

Concerto No. 2 in G Minor
L'Estate ("Summer")
I.

Allegro non molto

Languidezza per il caldo [Exhausted by the heat]
(A) *Sotto dura staggion' dal sole accesa Langue l'huom, langue 'l gregge,*

(Op. 8, No. 2 / RV 315)

ed arde il pino;

Allegro

Il cucco [The cuckoo]
(B) *Scioglie il cucco la voce, e tosto intesa*

19

Sopra il cantino

Allegro non molto

[The turtledove]
La tortorella
(C) *Canta la tortorella e 'l gardelino.*

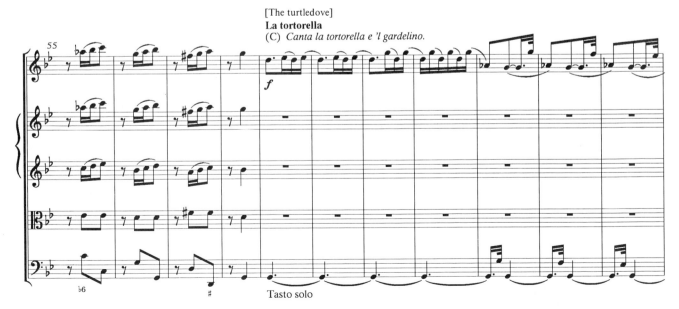

Tasto solo

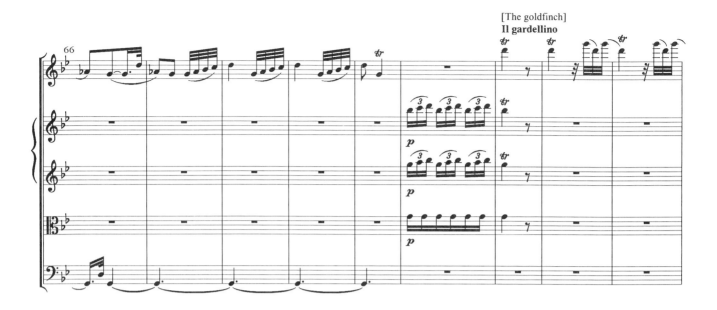

[The goldfinch]
Il gardellino

[Gentle breezes]
Zeffiretti dolci
(D) *Zeffiro dolce spira,*

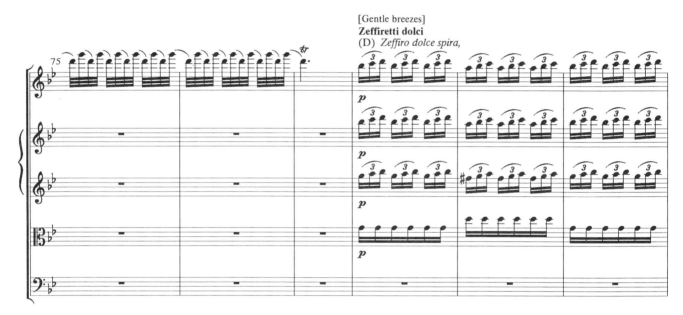

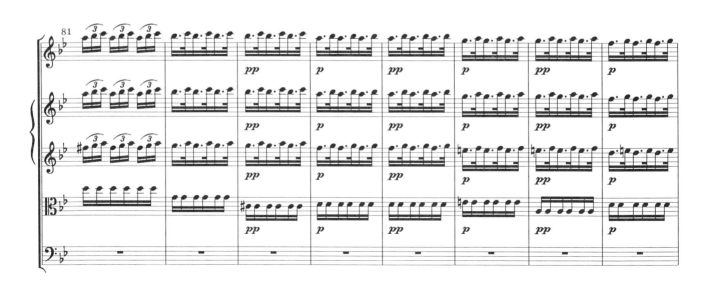

Vento Borea [The North Wind]
ma contesa   Muove Borea improviso al suo vicino;

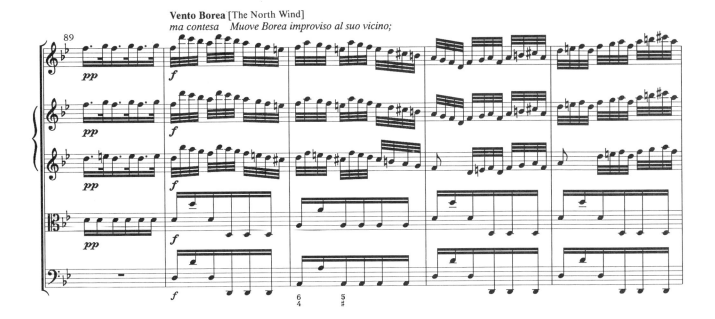

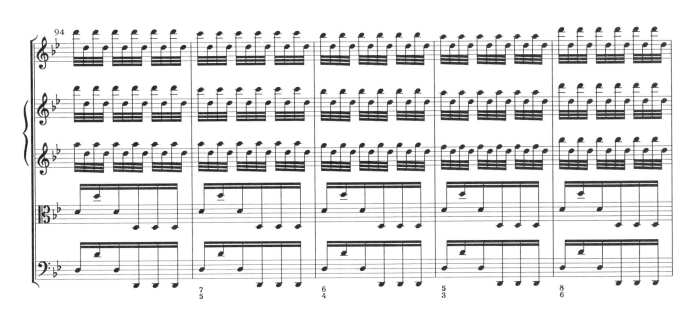

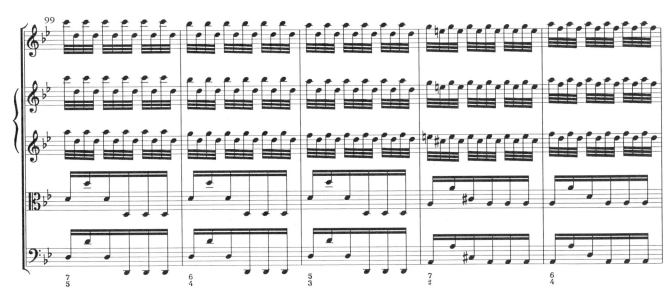

[The tears of the village boy]
Il pianto del villanello
(E) *E piange il pastorel, perchè sospesa*

Teme fiera borasca, e 'l suo destino.

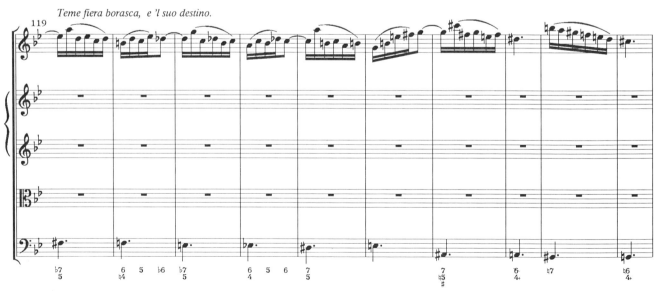

24   Concerto No. 2: *L'Estate*

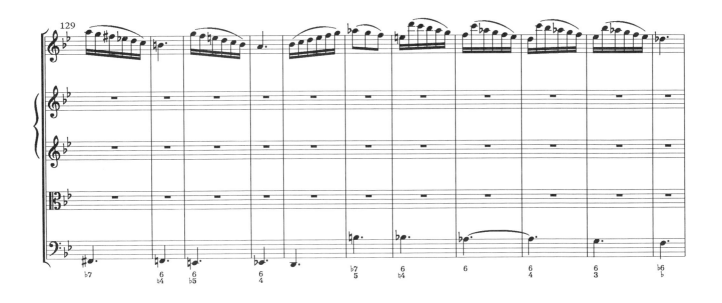

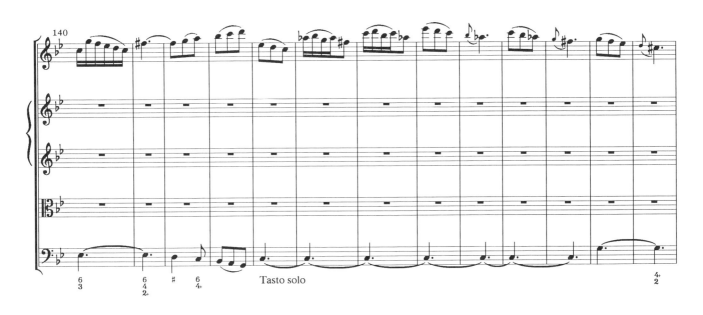

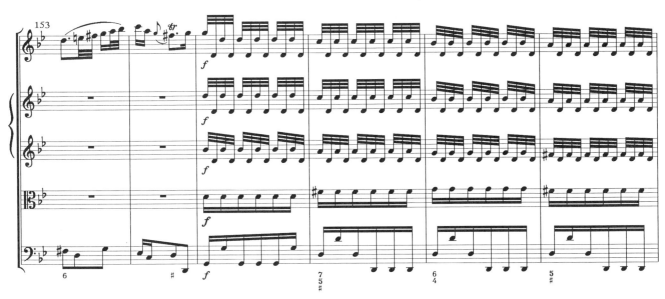

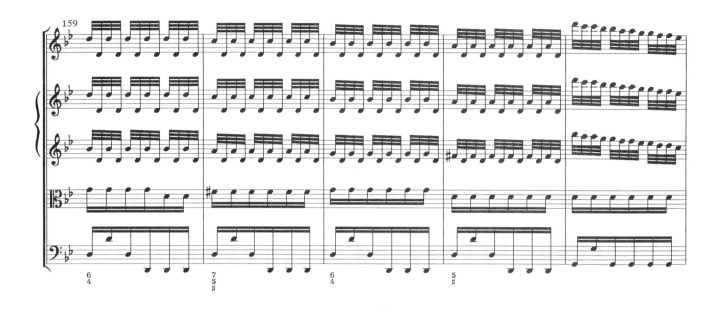

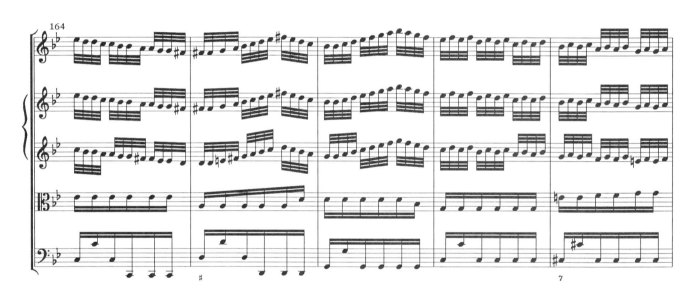

26   Concerto No. 2: *L'Estate*

II.

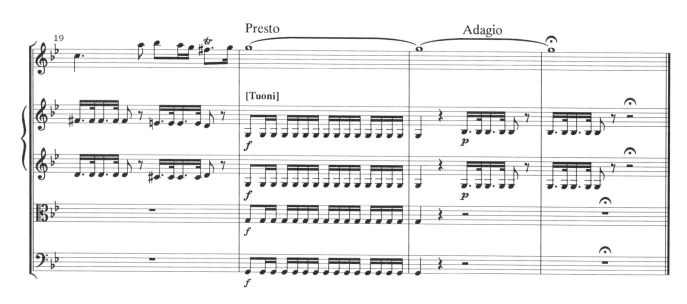

III.

Presto

Tempo impetuoso d'Estate [Summer's violent weather]
(G) *Ah, che pur troppo i suoi timor' son veri.*

Tuona e fulmina il Ciel,   *e grandinoso*

Tronca il capo alle spiche e a' grani alteri.

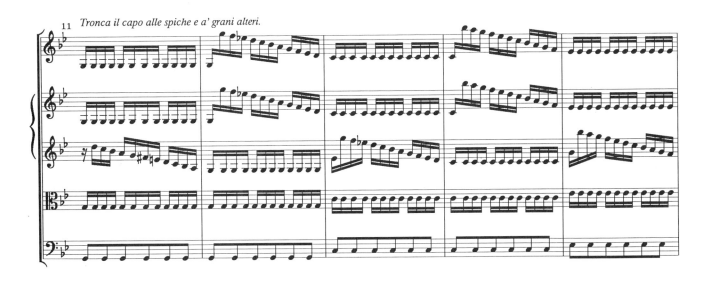

*For passages marked with an asterisk, see p. 226.

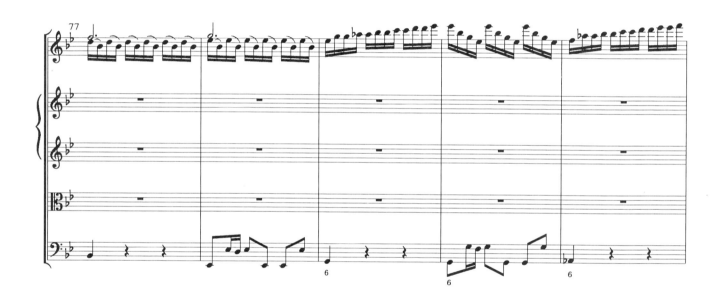

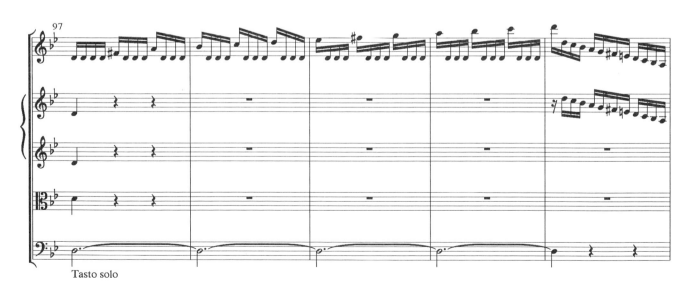

Tasto solo

Concerto No. 3 in F Major
L'Autunno ("Autumn")
I.

Allegro

Ballo e canto de' villanelli [Villagers' dance and song]
(A) *Celebra il vilanel con balli e canti   Del felice raccolto il bel piacere,*

(Op. 8, No. 3 / RV 293)

[The drunkard]
L'Ubriaco
(B) *E del liquor di*

Bacco accesi tanti

40   Concerto No. 3: *L'Autunno*

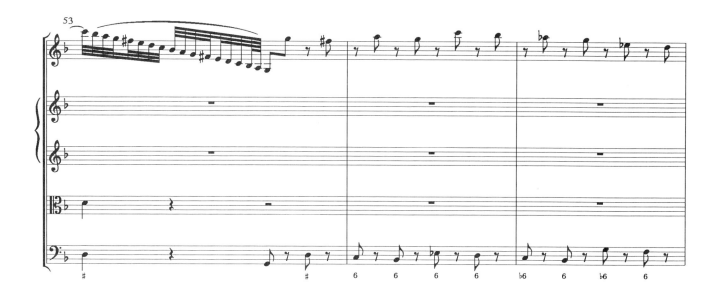

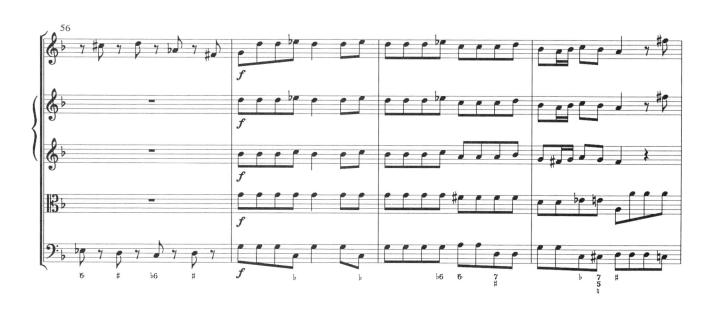

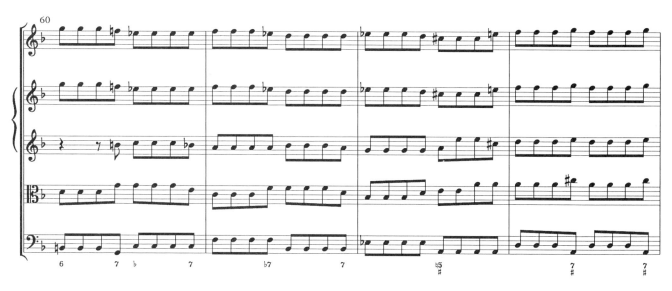

Larghetto [The dozing
L'Ubriaco che dorme drunkard]
(C) *Finiscono col sonno il lor godere.*

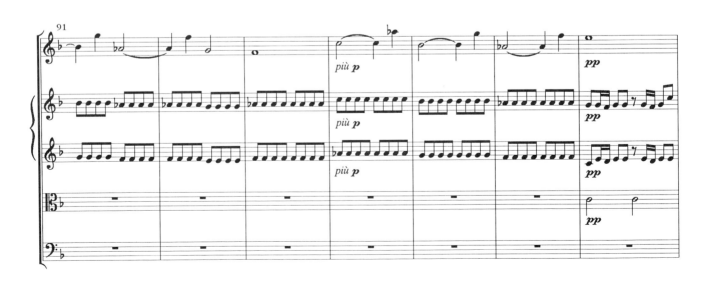

Allegro assai

II.

Ubriachi dormenti [Dozing drunkards]

(D) *Fa ch'ogn'uno tralasci e balli e canti, L'aria che temperata dà piacere.*

È la staggion ch'invita tanti e tanti D'un dolcissimo sonno al bel godere.

III.

Allegro

La caccia [The hunt]
(E) *I cacciator' alla nov'alba a caccia   Con corni, schioppi, e canni escono fuore.*

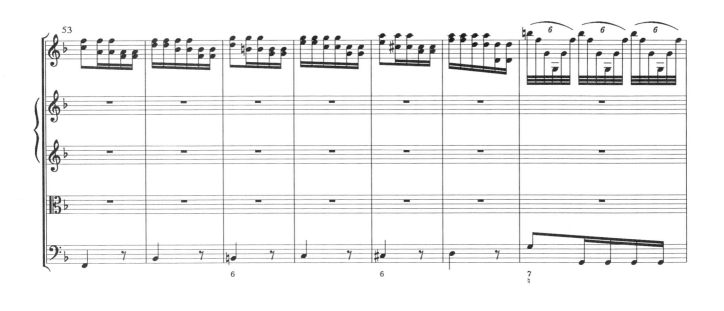

La fiera che fugge [The wild beast flees]
(F) *Fugge la belva, e seguono la traccia.*

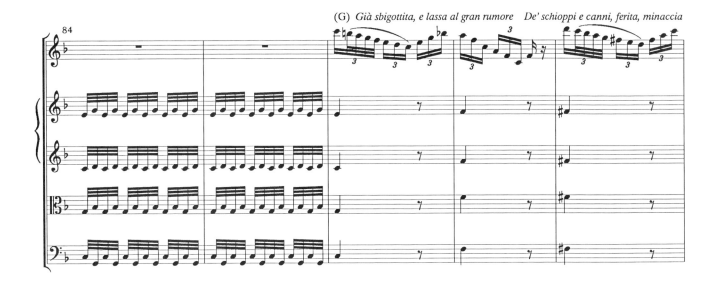

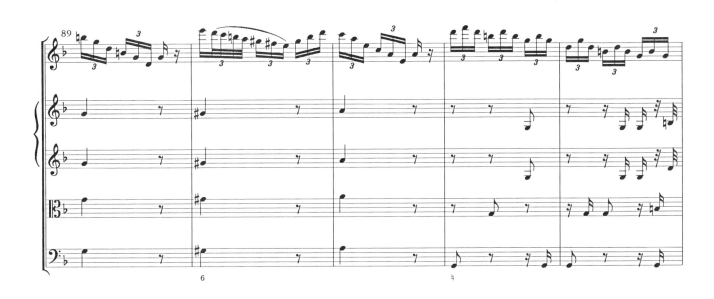

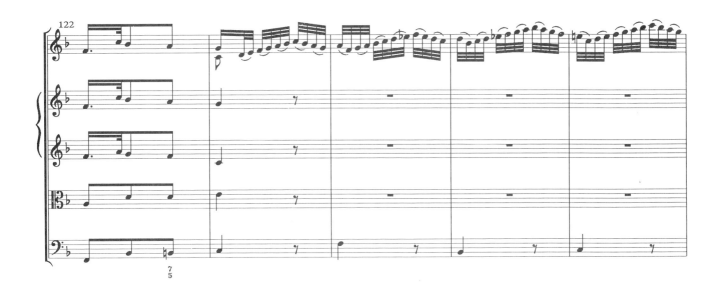

La fiera, fuggendo, muore [The beast, fleeing, dies]
(H) *Languida di fuggir, ma oppressa, muore.*

Tasto solo

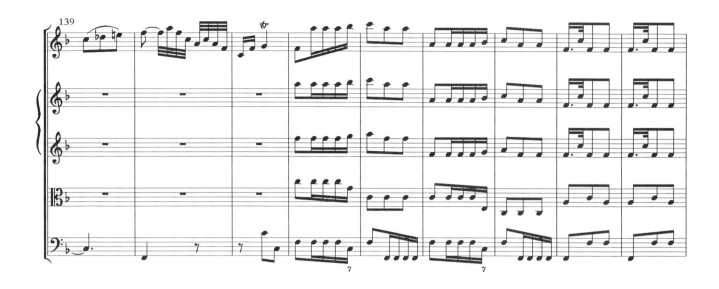

Concerto No. 4 in F Minor

L'Inverno ("Winter")

I.

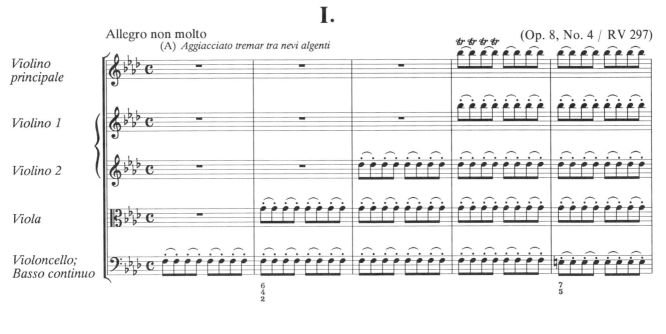

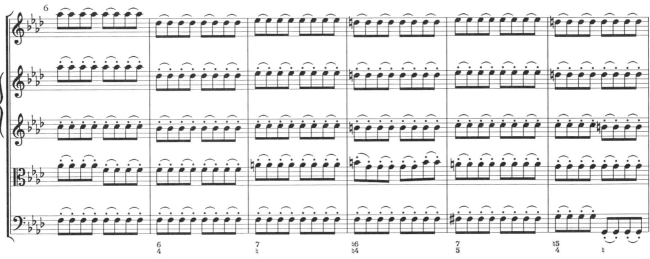

[Horrid wind]
Orrido vento
(B) *Al severo spirar d'orrido vento,*

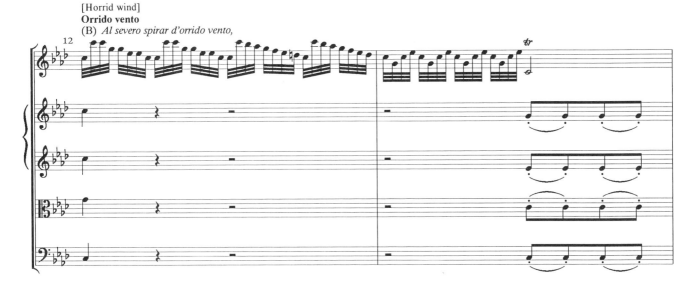

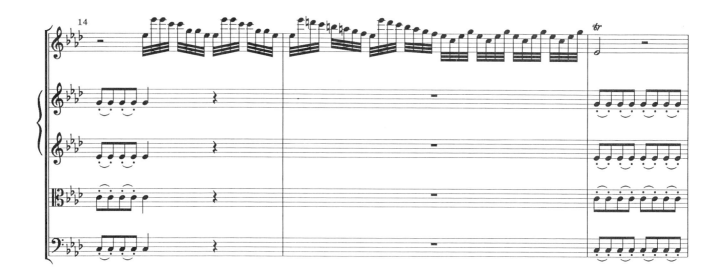

Batter de' piedi per
(C) *Correr battendo*

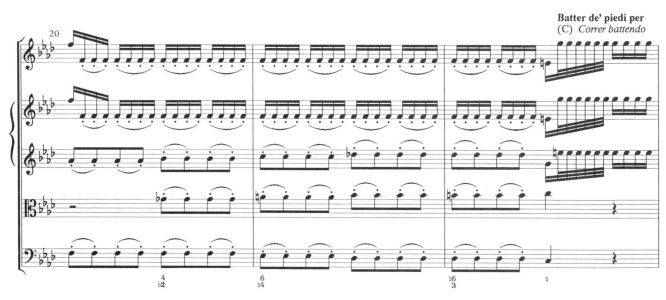

il freddo [To stamp one's feet from the cold]
i piedi ogni momento;

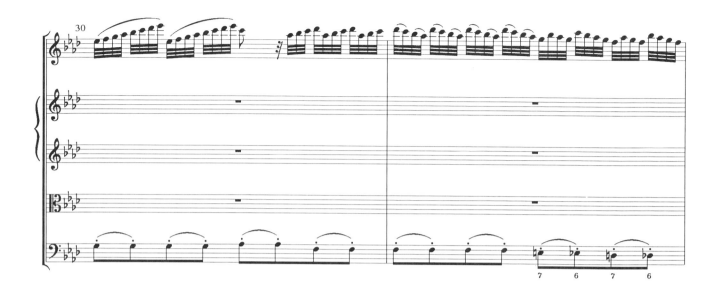

Venti [Winds]

Batter li denti [Chattering of teeth]
(D) *E pel soverchio gel batter i denti;*

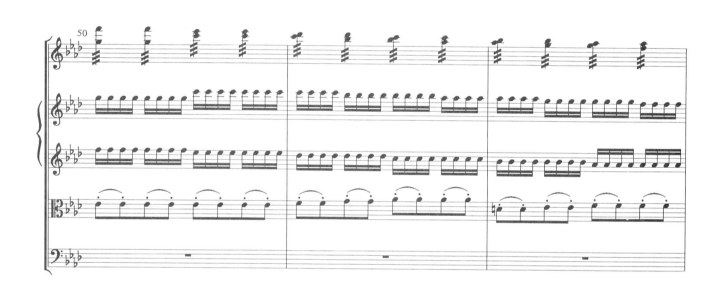

62   Concerto No. 4: *L'Inverno*

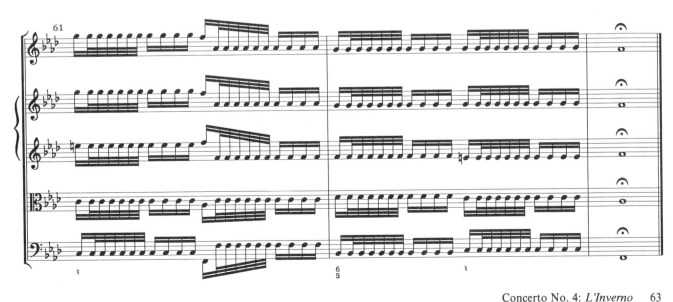

II.

La pioggia [The rain]

(E) *Passar al fuoco i dì quieti e contenti   Mentre la pioggia fuor bagna ben cento.*

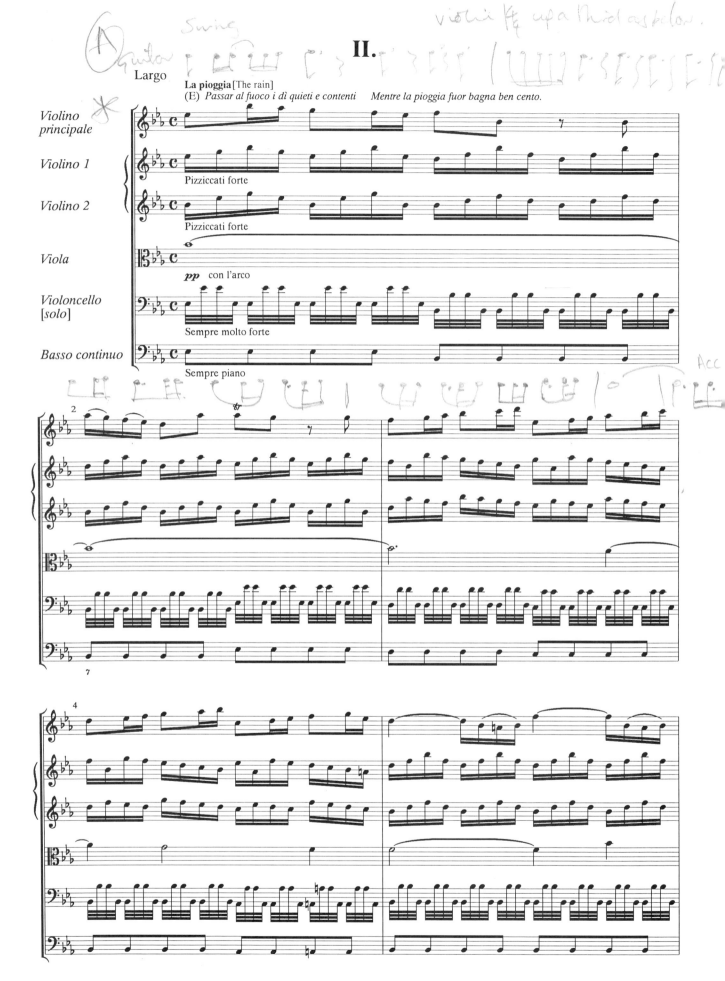

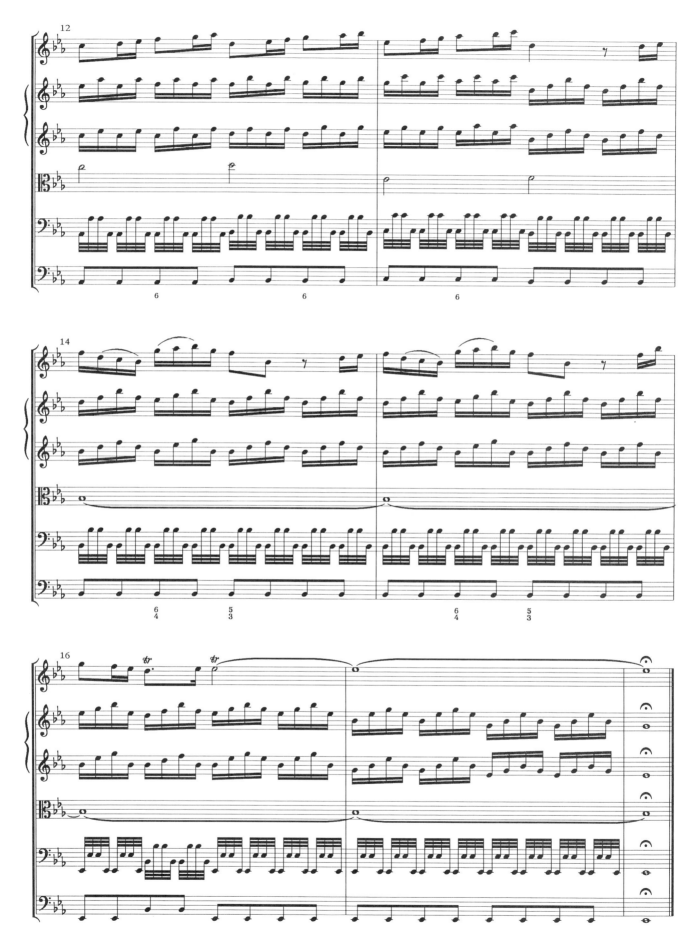

III.

Allegro

Violino principale

(F) *Caminar sopra 'l giaccio,*

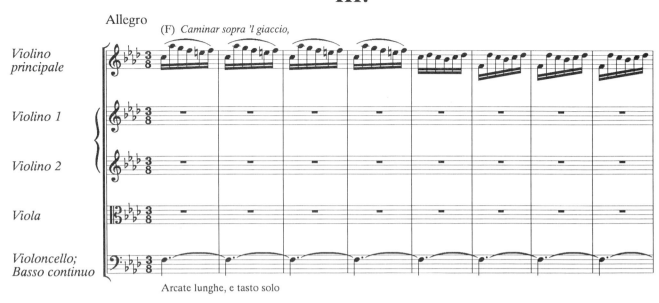

Violino 1

Violino 2

Viola

Violoncello;
Basso continuo

Arcate lunghe, e tasto solo

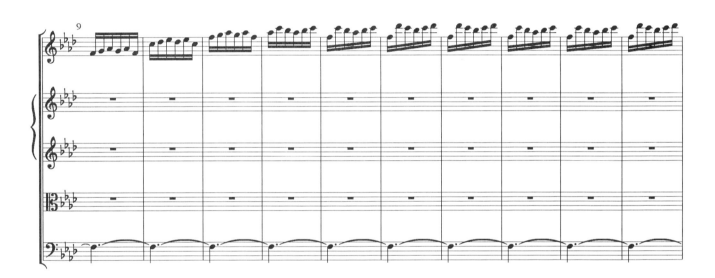

e a passo lento, (G) *Per timor di cader, girsene intenti.*

[Walking slowly and fearfully]
Caminar piano e con timore

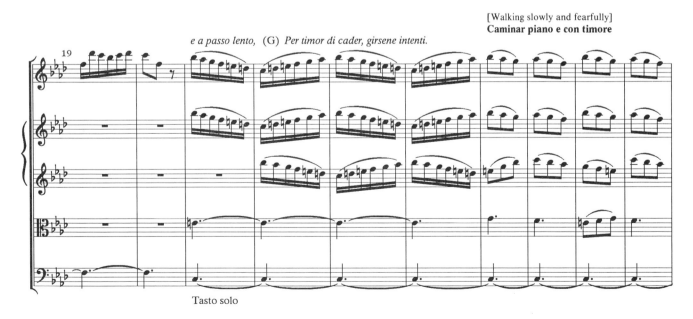

Tasto solo

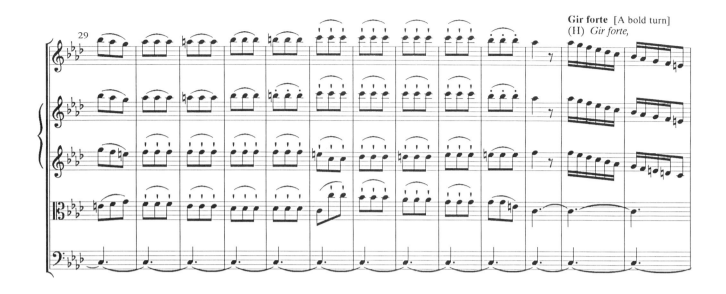

Gir forte [A bold turn]
(II) Gir forte,

sdruzziolar, cader a terra,

Cader a terra [Falling down]

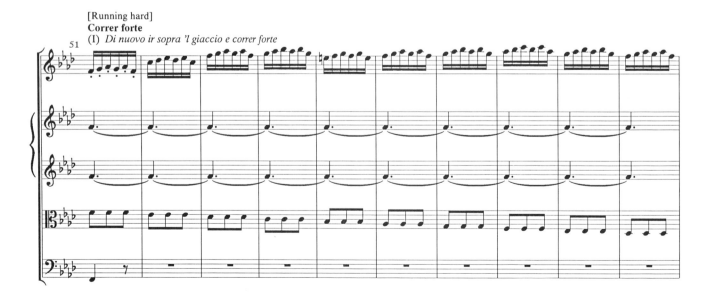

[Running hard]
Correr forte
(I) Di nuovo ir sopra 'l giaccio e correr forte

Tasto solo

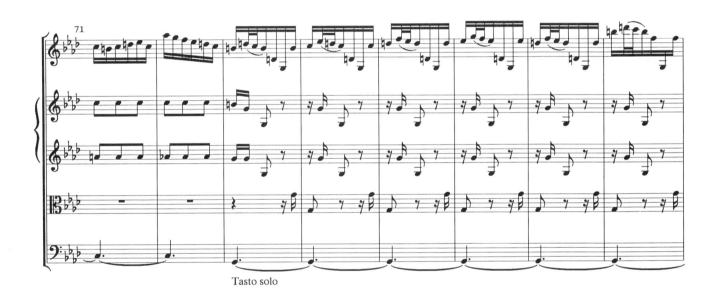

Tasto solo

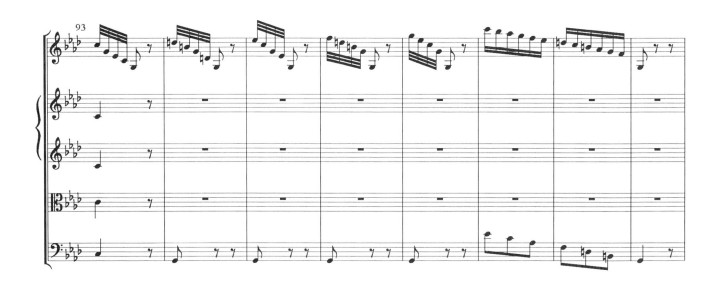

Lento

Il vento Sirocco [Sirocco (the hot desert wind)]
(M) *Sentir uscir dalle ferrate porte*

Il vento Borea

(N) *Sirocco, Borea, e tutti*

i venti in guerra.

e tutti li venti [and all the winds]

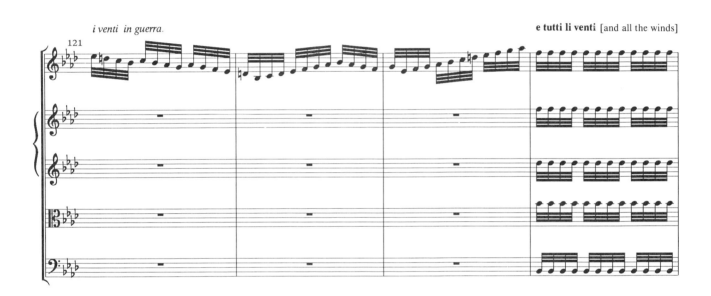

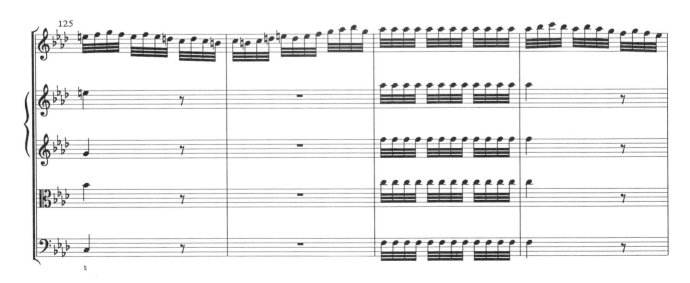

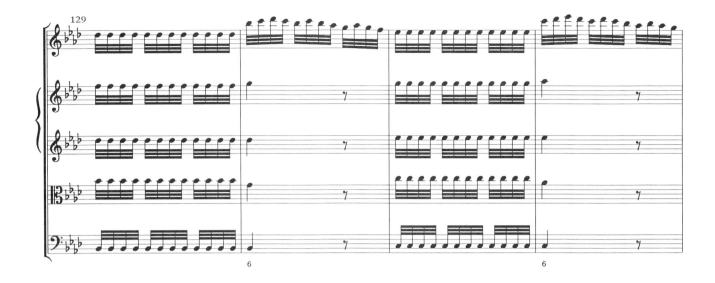

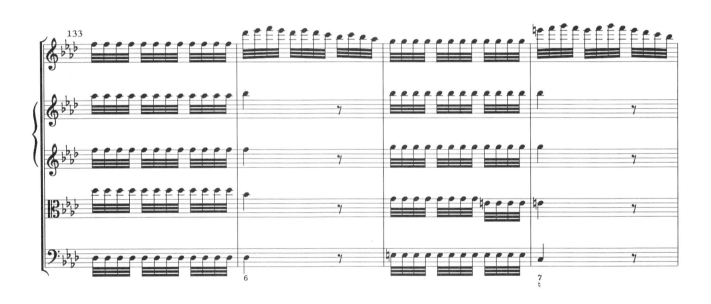

Quest'è 'l verno, ma tal che gioia

apporte.

Concerto No. 5 in E-flat Major

La Tempesta di Mare ("The Storm at Sea")

I.

Presto

(Op. 8, No. 5 / RV 253)

Violino
principale

Violino 1

Violino 2

Viola

Violoncello;
Basso continuo

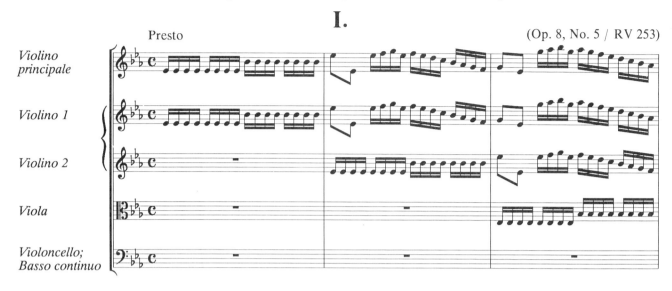

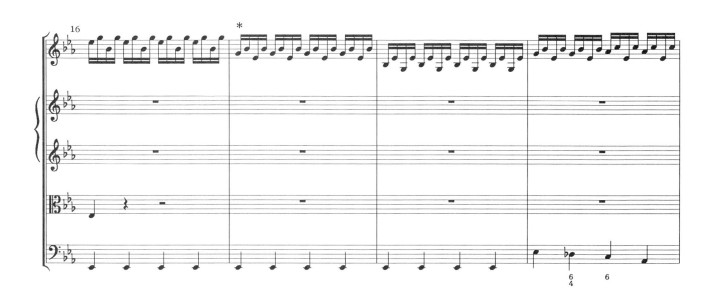

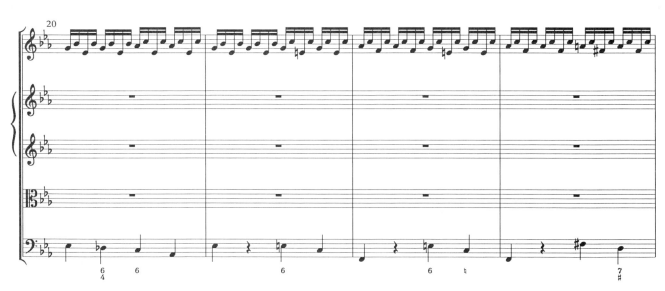

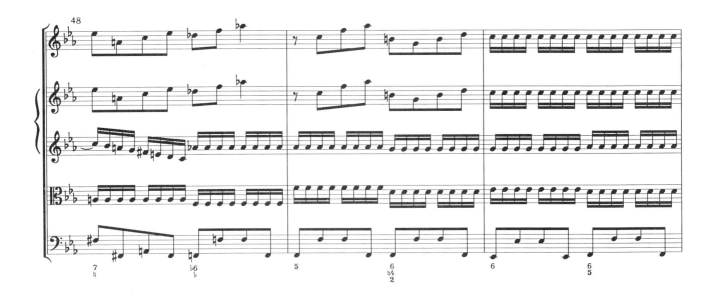

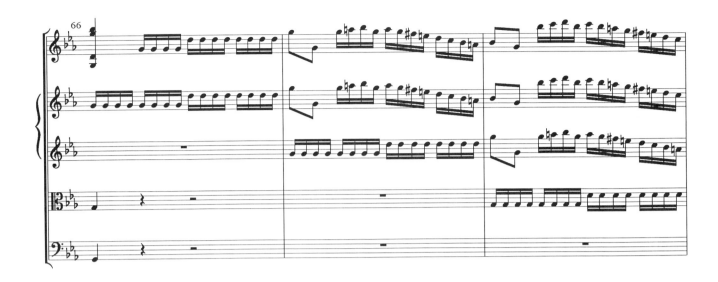

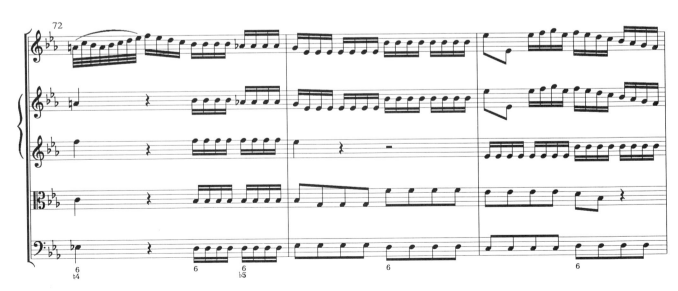

II.

Segue

III.

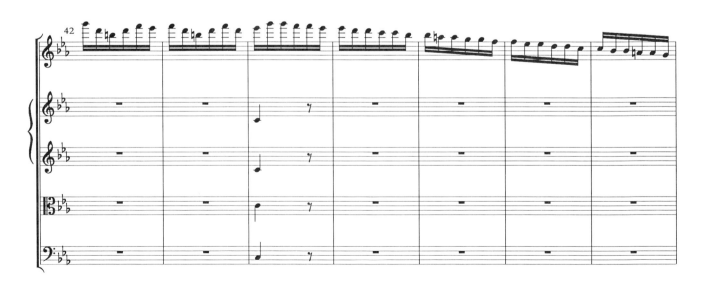

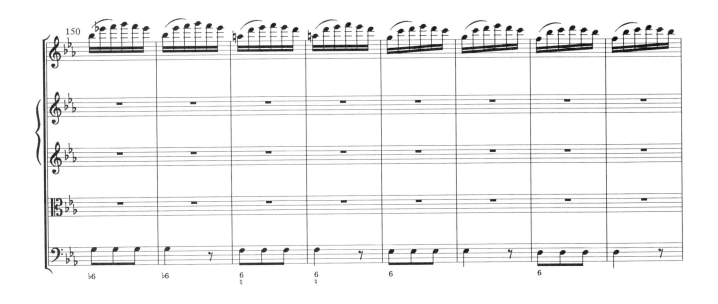

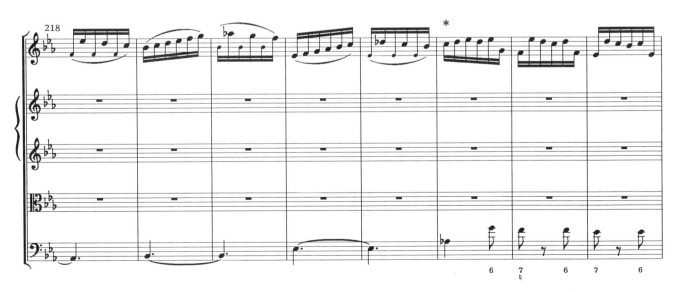

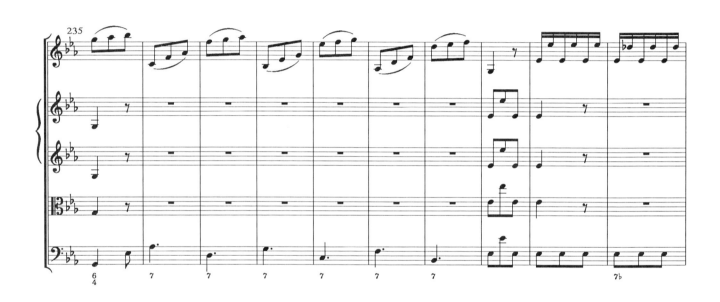

Concerto No. 6 in C Major

Il Piacere ("Pleasure")

I.

Allegro

(Op. 8, No. 6 / RV 180)

97

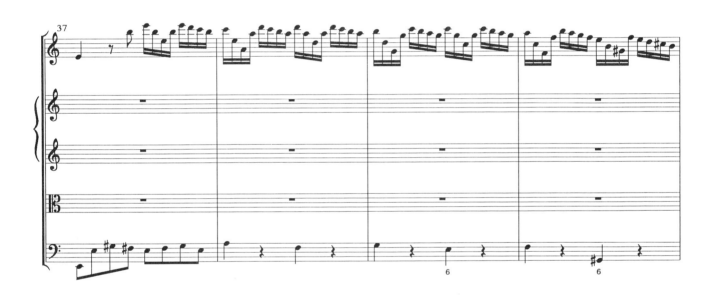

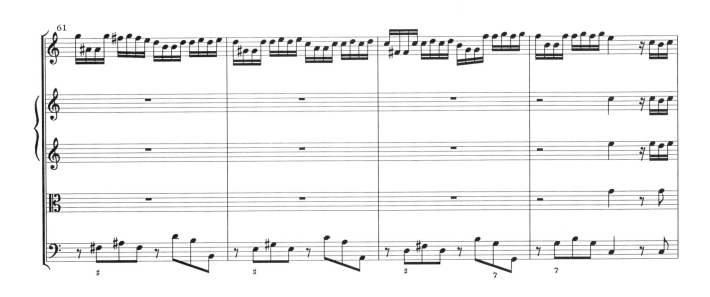

Tasto solo

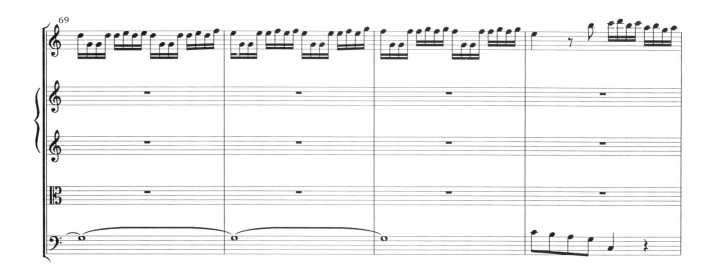

II.

Largo e cantabile

III.

Allegro

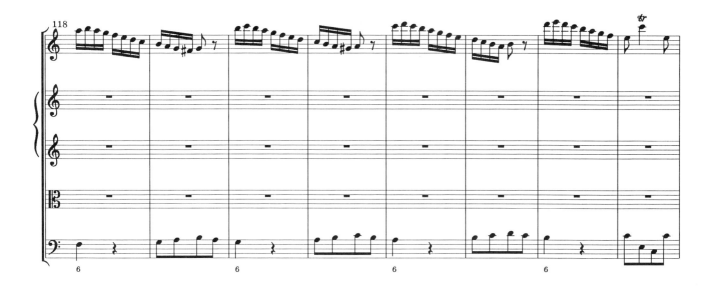

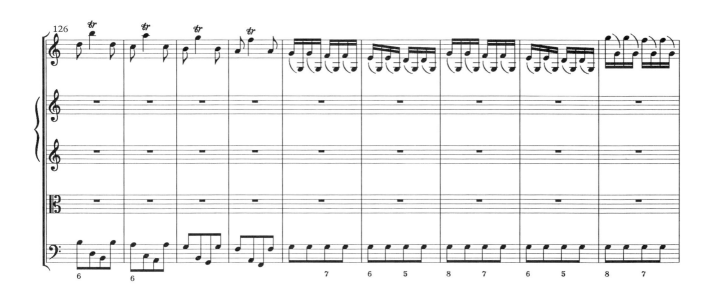

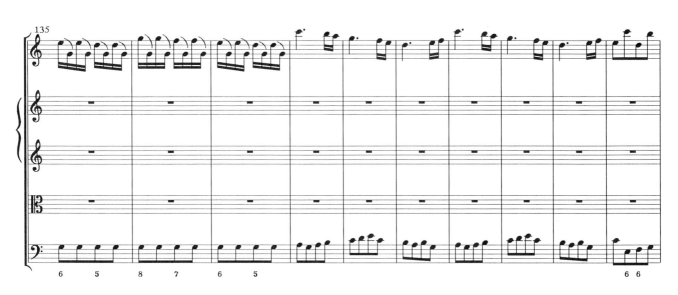

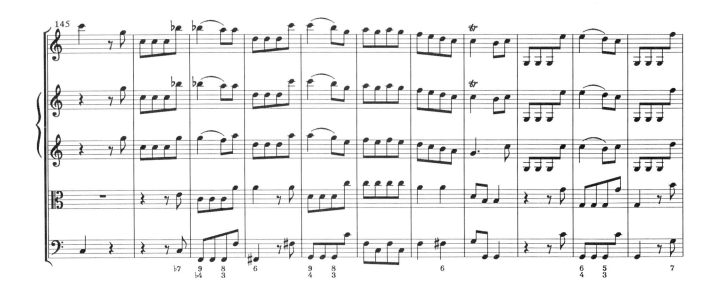

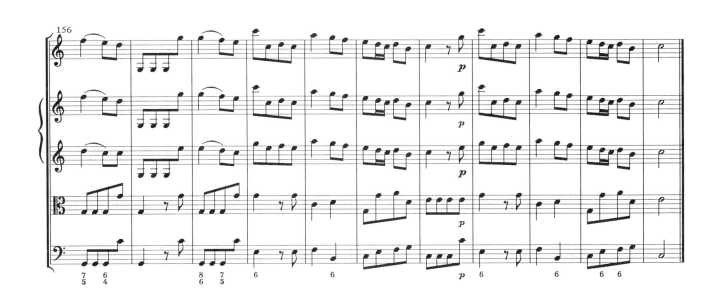

Concerto No. 7 in D Minor

I.

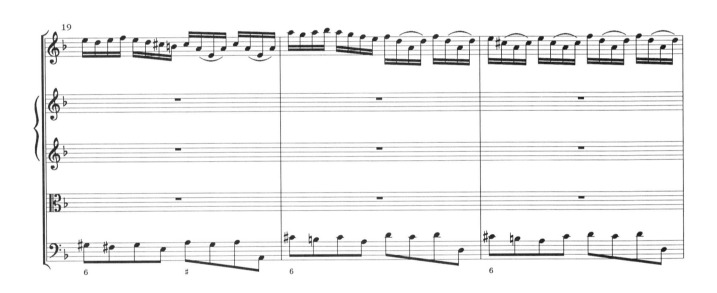

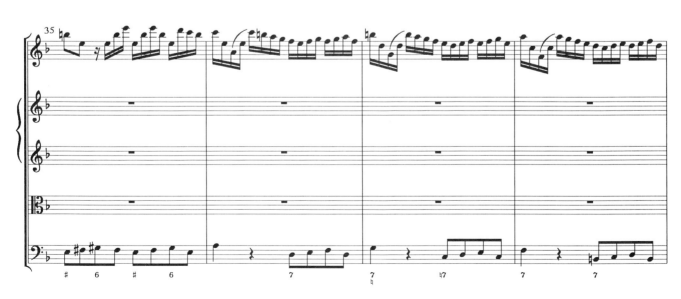

II.

III.

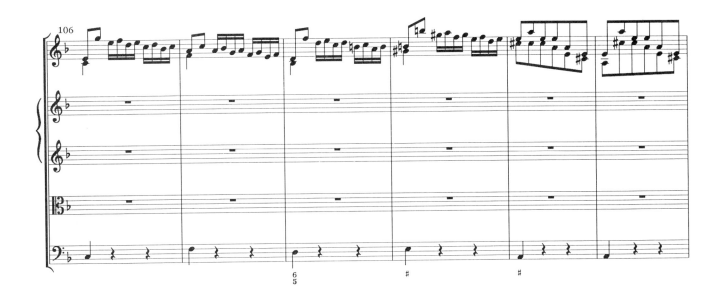

Concerto No. 8 in G Minor

I.

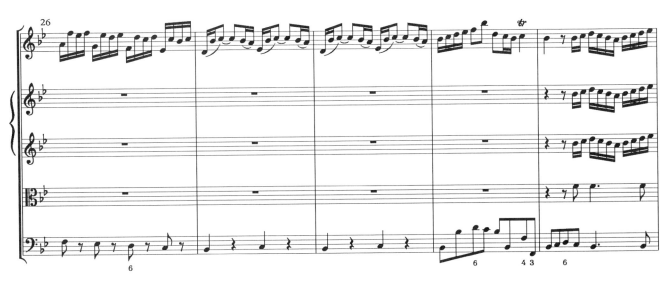

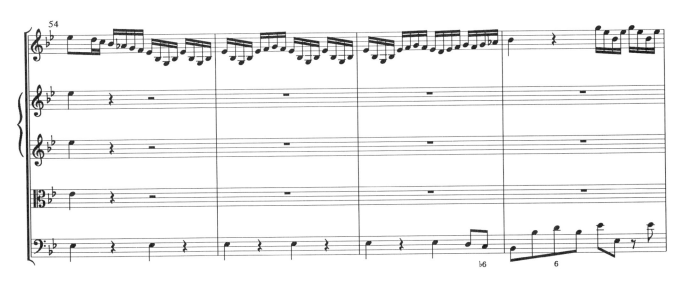

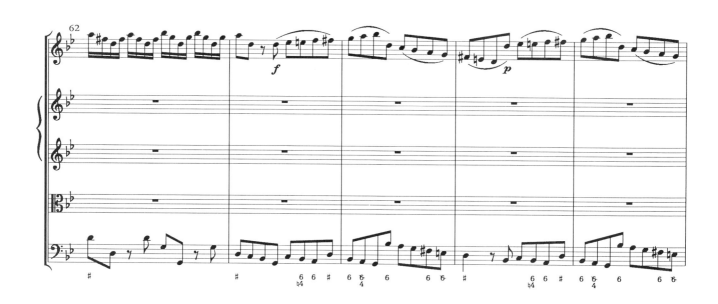

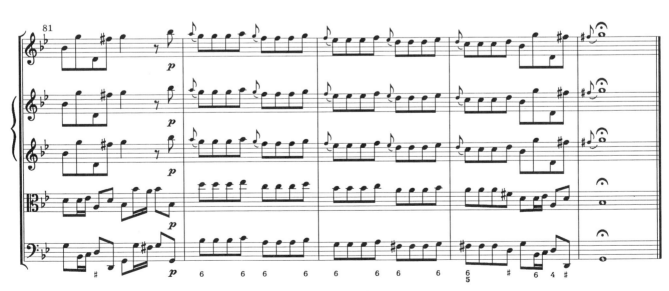

II.

III.

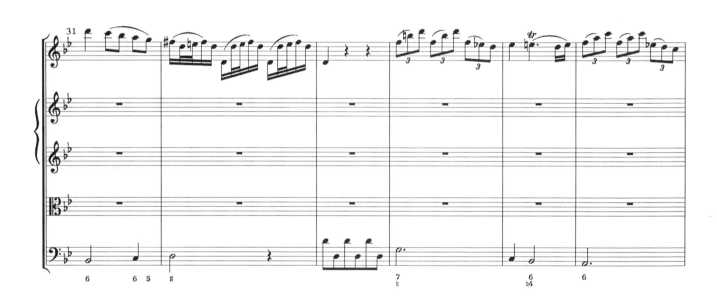

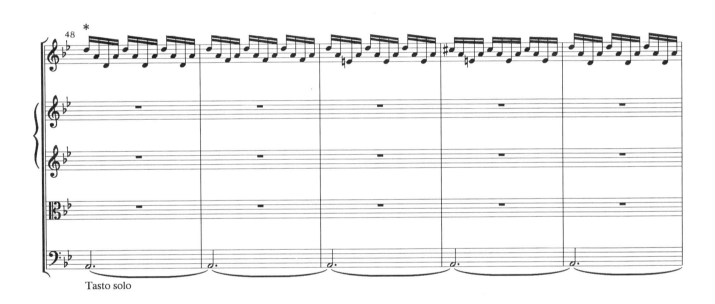

Tasto solo

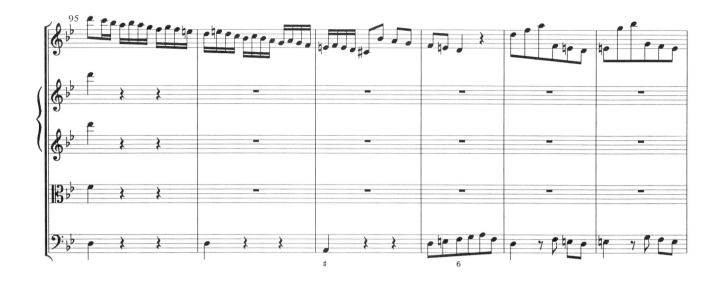

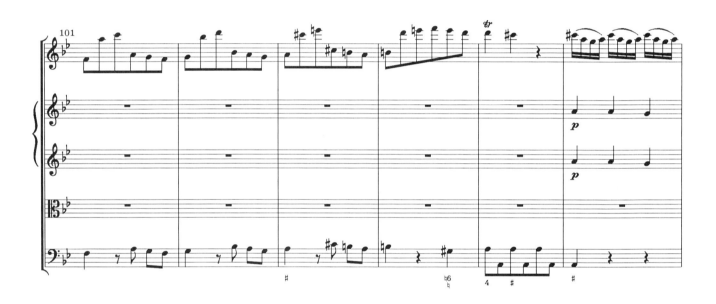

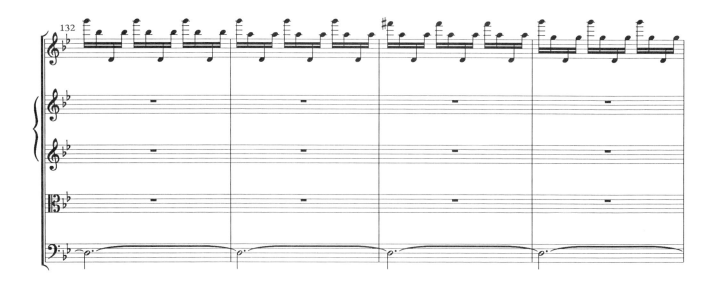

Concerto No. 9 in D Minor
I.

(Op. 8, No. 9 / RV 236)

II.

Largo

Violino principale

Violoncello;
Basso continuo

III.

Concerto No. 10 in B-flat Major

La Caccia ("The Hunt")

I.

(Op. 8, No. 10 / RV 362)

156   Concerto No. 10: *La Caccia*

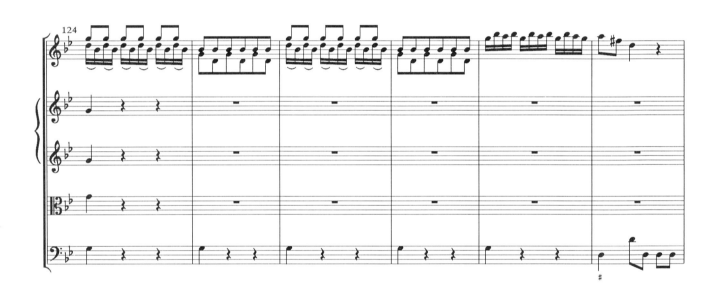

II.

III.

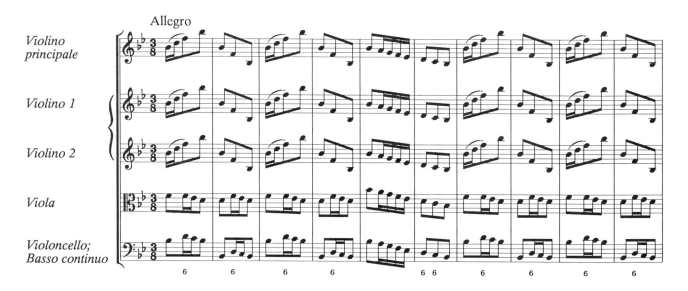

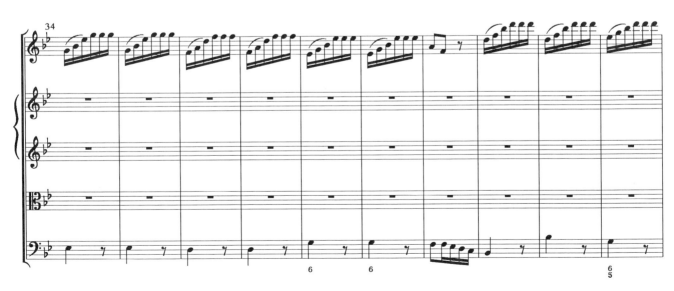

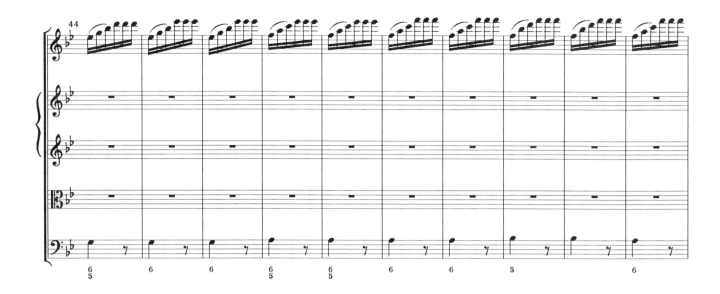

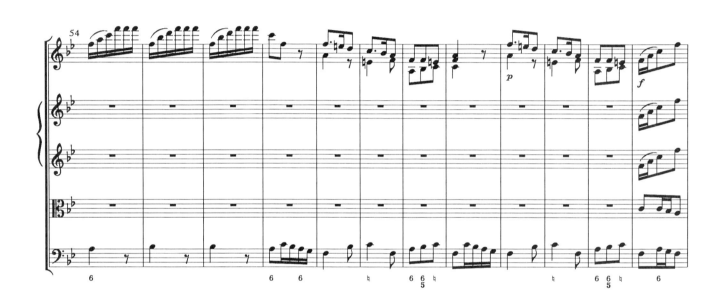

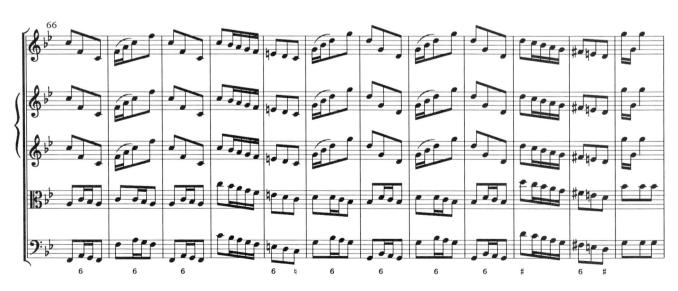

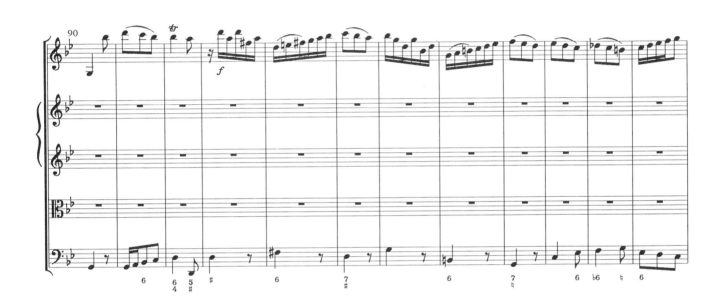

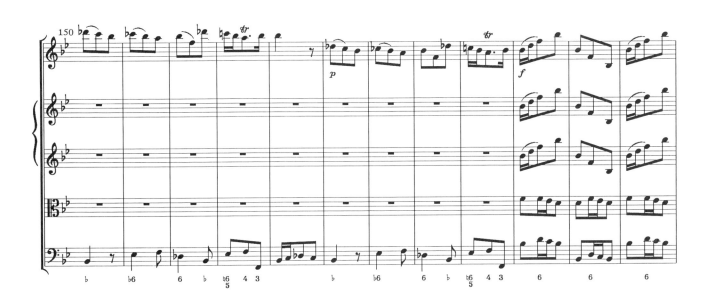

Concerto No. 11 in D Major
I.

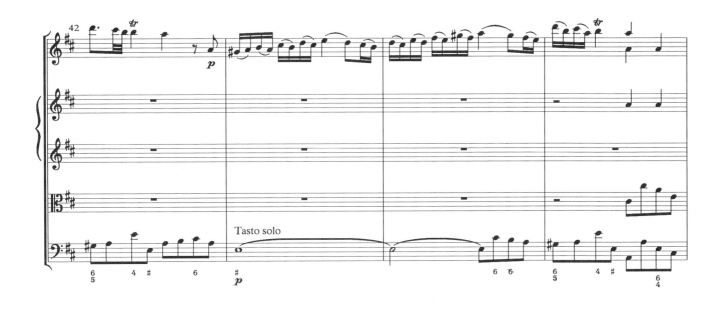

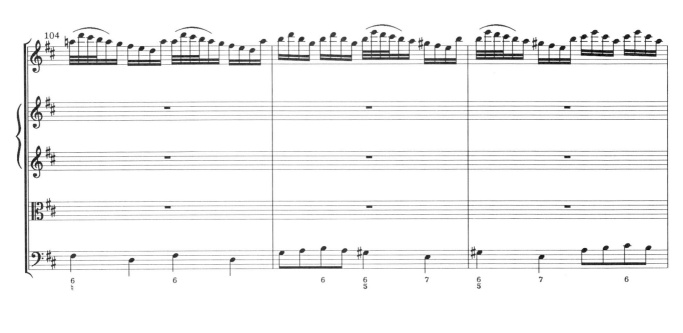

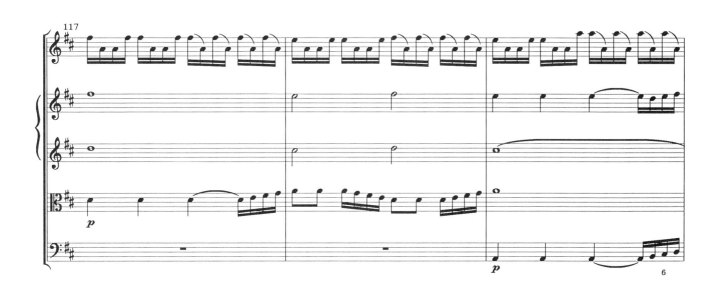

II.

III.

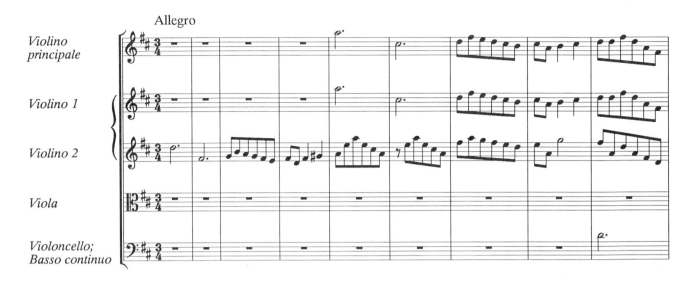

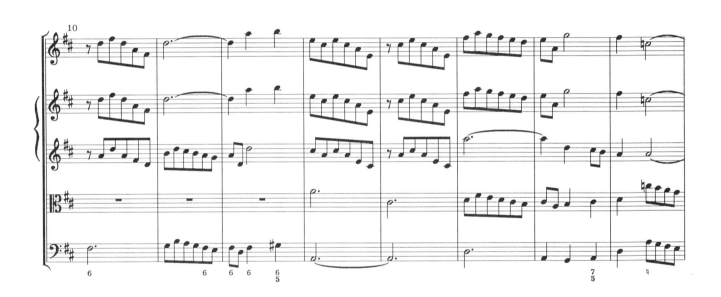

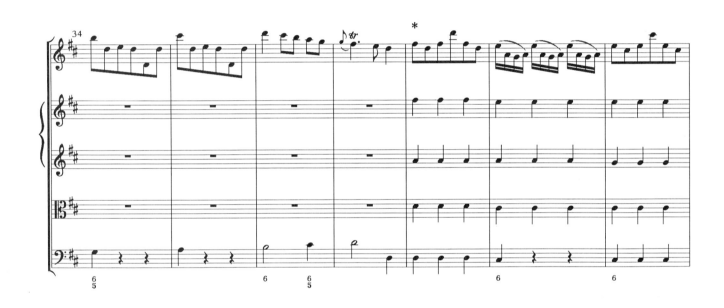

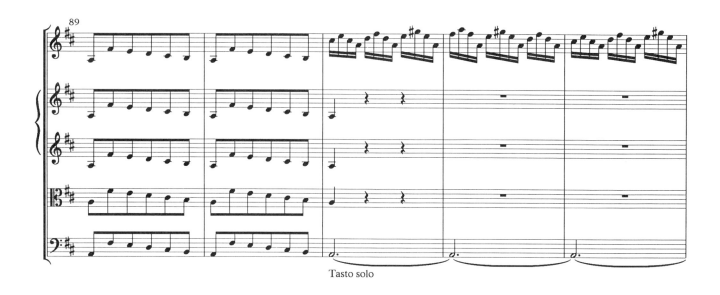

Tasto solo

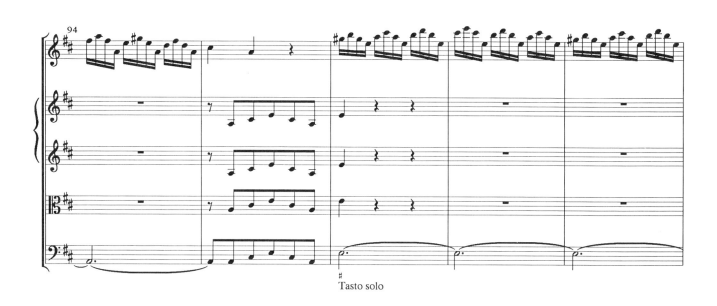

Tasto solo

Concerto No. 12 in C Major

I.

Allegro

(Op. 8, No. 12 / RV 178)

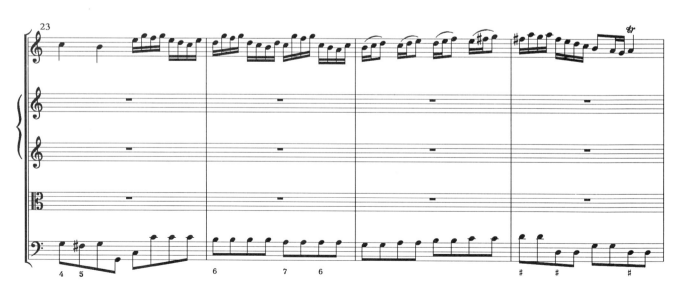

II.

III.

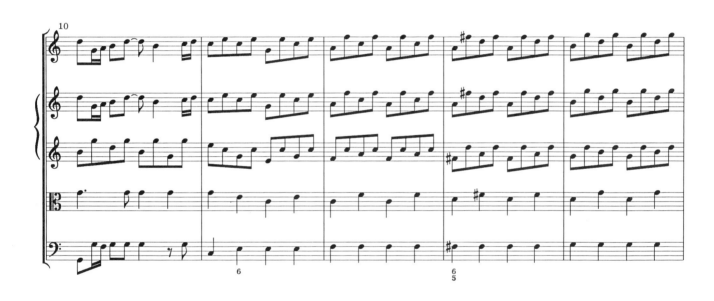

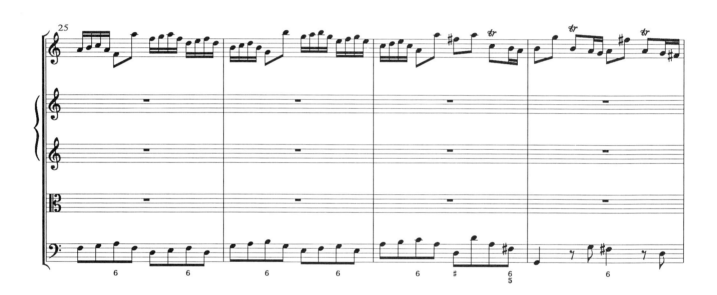

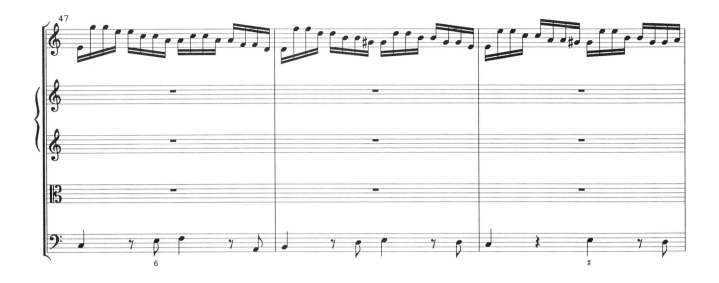

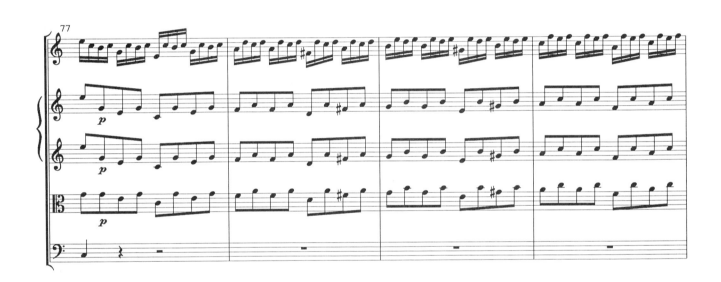

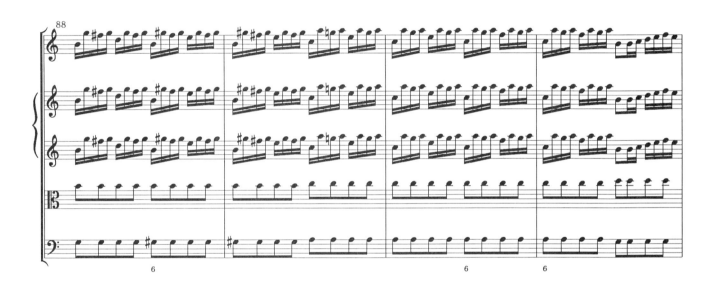

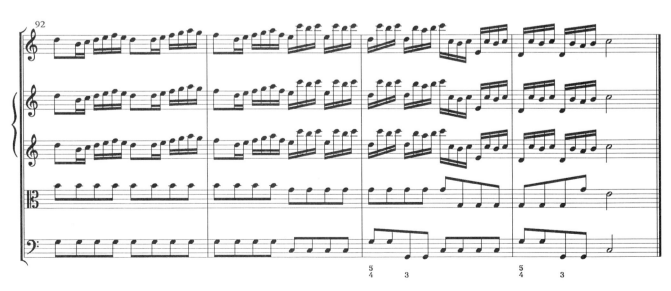

IMPORTANT VARIANTS

HOW TO USE THE VARIANTS

Vivaldi's autographs support the creation of new versions of some of the works of Opus 8. Instructions to assemble these alternative versions are given below. The alternative musical passages follow.

No. 7. To create an alternative version, change one solo in the first movement to use the substitute Bars 50-76 found on pp. 209-10.

No. 9. The oboe concerto differs from the violin concerto principally in using an alternative solo in Bars 91-108. This solo is found on p. 211.

No. 11. There are a number of possible versions of this work. They can be constructed by substituting various materials found on pp. 212-219. The standing material in this edition represents Vivaldi's original manuscript version, insofar as it can be determined. The principal variant is Version 2.

To assemble the first movement of Version 2, proceed as follows:

Bar Nos.	Instructions
$1-100^2$	Use standing material
100^3-112^4	Substitute Variant 11a, Bars 100^3-126^4
113^1-121^4	Use standing material (as Bars 127^1-135^4)
122^1-132^2	Substitute Variant 11b, Bars 122^1-129^2 (as Bars 136^1-143^2)
132^3-137	Use standing material (as Bars 143^3-148)

To assemble the third movement of Version 2, proceed as follows:

Bar Nos.	Instructions
1-37	Use standing material
38-67	Substitute Variant 11c, Bars 38-67
68-112	Use standing material
113-154	Substitute Variant 11d, Bars 113-139
155-170	Use standing material (as Bars 140-155)
171-214	Substitute Variant 11e, 8 bars (as Bars 156-163)

Version 3 is the same as Version 2 through Bar 170 of the third movement of Version 1 (= Bar 155 of Version 2). The completion of this movement offers a range of possibilities. Bar numbers cited outside parentheses below and on pp. 218 and 219 are consistent with those found on pp. 186-88. Actual bar numbers vary with the version created. The options are described below:

Bar Nos.	Instructions
171-208	1a. Substitute the 5-bar passage sketched on p. 238 (as Bars 156-160) OR 1b. Proceed to Step 2b 2a. Use Variant 11f (with a one-bar overlap, as Bars 160-197) OR 2b. Use Variant 11f (as Bars 156-193)
209-214	3a. Use 11e (as Bars 198-205 or as Bars 194-201) OR 3b. Use its 7-bar variant on p. 238 (as Bars 198-204 or as Bars 194-200)

The possibilities thus obtained are:

Version 3a	1a + 2a + 3a	205 bars total
Version 3b	1a + 2a + 3b	204 bars total
Version 3c	(1b) + 2b + 3a	201 bars total
Version 3d	(1b) + 2b + 3b	200 bars total

Concerto No. 7 in D Minor
Mvmt. I: Version 2

Variant 7a: Substitute for Bars 50–76

Concerto No. 9 in D Minor
Version for Oboe, Strings and Continuo
(RV 454): Mvmt. I

Variant 9a: Substitute for Bars 91–102

Go to Bar 103, p. 146

Concerto No. 11 in D Major
Mvmt. I: Version 2

Variant 11a: Substitute for Bars 100–112

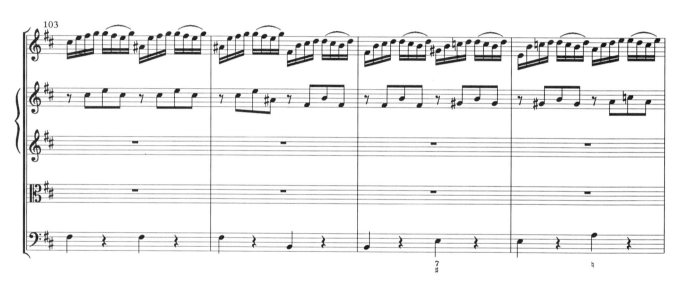

Go to Bar 113, p. 175

Concerto No. 11 in D Major
Mvmt. I: Version 2

Variant 11b: Substitute for Bars 122–132

Violino principale

Violino 1

Violino 2

Go to Bar 132³, p. 176

Concerto No. 11 in D Major
Mvmt. III: Version 2

Variant 11c: Substitute for Bars 38–67

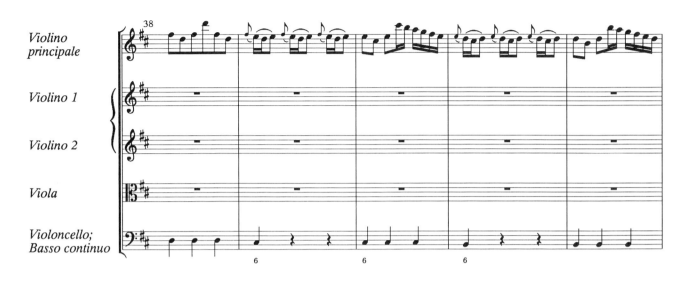

Go to Bar 68, p. 181

Concerto No. 11 in D Major
Mvmt. III: Version 2

Variant 11d: Substitute for Bars 113-154

Go to Bar 155, p. 186

Concerto No. 11 in D Major
Mvmt. III: Version 2

Variant 11e: Substitute for Bars 171–214

Concerto No. 11 in D Major
Mvmt. III: Version 3

Variant 11f: Substitute for Bars 171–208

Go to Variant 11e, p. 218

CRITICAL NOTES

THE SOURCES

The four chief sources for the concertos of Op. 8 are the print made in Amsterdam in 1725 by Michel-Charles Le Cène and three incomplete sets of manuscripts found in Dresden (Germany), Turin (Italy) and Manchester (England). A specific listing of the contents of these sources is given on p. 225.

THE AMSTERDAM PRINT (1725)

Like many Dutch prints of Italian music, the published versions of these works contain many small defects, such as inconsistencies in the rendering of parts that are musically parallel. Truly incorrect pitches are found at a relatively low level, although haphazardly marked accidentals are numerous. Rhythmic errors are few. The instrumental parts are identified as *Violino principale*, *Violino primo*, *Violino secondo*, *Alto viola*, and *Organo e Violoncello*. These designations are retained in three Parisian reprints—of *c.*1739, 1743, and 1748—all by Charles-Nicolas Le Clerc, a violinist turned publisher.

The more daunting questions that arise from these prints are those of authority. Because Op. 8 carries a dedication written by Vivaldi, we can be sure that this publication was sanctioned by the composer. It seems unlikely that he saw proof copy, however. "The Four Seasons" had a substantial performance history prior to publication and thus the copies offered for print, even if inadequately proofread, are highly polished musically. One exception, however, is the elusive obbligato *Violoncello* part of the slow movement of the "Winter" concerto, which is missing from many modern editions and recordings. It is incorporated in this edition. Discrepancies between parts are widespread, especially in the dynamics and placement of text elements in "The Four Seasons."

Many of the remaining works that make up Op. 8 seem not to have had the benefit of frequent performance. While some works—especially No. 5 ("The Tempest") and No. 10 ("The Hunt")—give, like "The Four Seasons," evidence of currency in the repertory of the time, other numbers may not have been performed prior to publication. In the case of No. 9, for example, the performed version may have been that for oboe (preserved in manuscript) rather than that for violin, an adaptation intended to appeal to a broader market. Abrupt transitions are occasionally found in some of the other concertos of this collection and many contain unison ritornellos that amount to little more than sketches in Vivaldi's autographs. In the case of No. 11, manuscript sources suggest either that Vivaldi never settled on a final version of the work or that he adapted the solo episodes to suit a series of different violinists. The work printed by Le Cène may represent a preliminary selection of draft material.

THE DRESDEN MANUSCRIPTS

The manuscript materials preserved in Dresden include scores and parts (not necessarily for the same works). The most valuable of these are the copies made by Johann Georg Pisendel, a famous violinist of Vivaldi's time, who visited Venice in 1716. Pisendel became an important exponent of Vivaldi's music at the Saxon court in Dresden, where he led the orchestra from 1730 to 1755. He was especially noted for his execution of expressive slow movements.

In the case of Op. 8, the greatest differences from the Amsterdam print concern the treatment of the *Violino principale* and *Basso continuo* parts. In the *Violino principale* the slurs are often longer and differently articulated from those of the print. Since the Pisendel manuscripts are earlier than or contemporary with the print, we must regard them as more authoritative in these matters. The *Basso continuo* tends to be more fully articulated rhythmically and more clearly differentiated from the *Violoncello* than in the Amsterdam print. Although these differences may have been influenced by Saxon practice, bowings and many virtuoso details have been adopted in this edition. Continuo figuration is far more extensive in these manuscripts, and often more accurate, than in the Amsterdam print. Fermatas on final notes, which appear only haphazardly in the print, are ubiquitous in these and the other manuscript sets.

THE MANCHESTER PARTBOOKS

These partbooks were probably copied in Rome around the time of Vivaldi's death. They show many evidences of use and are valuable for their consistency (generally followed in this edition) in the use of slurs and ties. Many notes that are wrong or ambiguous in the print are appropriately corrected. Continuo figuration is fuller and more accurately placed than in the Amsterdam print. The sonnet texts for "The Four Seasons" are not given in these parts, but the letters that link them with the musical structure are retained. The placement of labels varies between parts. The *Viola* part is labelled *Violetta*.

Since these manuscripts apparently accommodated Roman performance practice, their prescriptions—for example, in the variable instrumentation of the *Basso continuo*—do not necessarily represent Vivaldi's thinking. Some of the more interpretive changes have not been accepted. Among the elements generally rejected are (1) trills or staccatos substituted for detached legato and martellato markings, and other changes to Vivaldi's articulation; (2) harmonies changed from minor to major; (3) cadential tones altered to "complete" Vivaldi's harmony, where he has omitted a third or a fifth; (4) changes of texture in the inner parts; and (5) transpositions of an octave in the *Basso continuo*.

THE TURIN AUTOGRAPH SCORES

Vivaldi's autograph scores in Turin, which constitute the largest surviving corpus of his music, are extremely valuable. They provide insight into both Vivaldi's methods of composition and his technical solutions to performance problems. In these sources the variability of Vivaldi's own thought on musical construction can be clearly seen. It is apparent that he often fashioned his solos and harmonic schemes first and then left the realization of ritornellos to copyists. For this reason, the sources do not always agree on the presence or absence of the ripieno string parts in interior passages. Vivaldi sometimes substituted new solo episodes (Nos. 7 and 11). For the printed version of Nos. 9 and 12, the principal instrument was changed from oboe to violin. Alternative readings of Nos. 7, 9 and 11 can be created by substituting the Important Variants for standing materials. Rhythmic detail is often more articulate in Vivaldi's manuscripts than in the print or other copies. The rhythmic detail of the opening motive of No. 10, "The Hunt," offers a striking example.

In solo episodes some of the Turin manuscripts include position numbers for certain notes and a wealth of other subtlety in the management of what was, for its day, a dauntingly difficult repertory for the virtuoso. Vivaldi's method of assisting other performers is rarely reflected in modern editions; some examples of this effort are indicated in the Table of Emendations.

PRINCIPAL SOURCES
FOR THE CONCERTOS, OP. 8, NOS. 1–12

Amsterdam Print (A)	Dresden Manuscripts (D)	Manchester Manuscripts (M)	Turin Manuscripts (T)
No. 1 RV 269		GB-Mp MS 580 Ct 51, vv. 1-4, 6; No. 9: copy of A	
No. 2 RV 315		GB-Mp MS 580 Ct 51, vv. 1-4, 6; No. 10: copy of A	
No. 3 RV 293		GB-Mp MS 580 Ct 51, vv. 1-4, 6; No. 11: copy of A	
No. 4 RV 297		GB-Mp MS 580 Ct 51, vv. 1-4, 6; No. 12: copy of A	
No. 5 RV 253	D-Dlb MS 2389-O-62: parts in the hand of Pisendel and later scribes	GB-Mp MS 580 Ct 51, vv. 1-4, 6; No. 13: copy of A	
No. 6 RV 180			
No. 7 RV 242	D-Dlb 2389-O-44: autograph score for first movement		
No. 8 RV 332			MS. Giordano 30, No. 1, ff. 2-11: autograph score
No. 9 RV 236 Oboe version = RV 454			MS. Foà 32, No. 6, ff. 41- 50: autograph score (as oboe concerto)
No. 10 RV 362	D-Dlb 2389-O-63: parts		MS. Giordano 29, No. 28, ff. 245-53: autograph score
No. 11 RV 210			MS. Giordano 30, No. 25, ff. 184-206; + Giordano 29, f. 304: autograph score with myriad revisions
No. 12 RV 178 Oboe version = RV 449			

THE DOVER EDITION

The vast majority of editions and recordings of all of these works are based on the Amsterdam print. This edition, which is intended to serve both as a study score for listeners and as a reference score for performers, is based on a comparative reading of all the sources listed on the preceding page and seeks to provide the best reading. Ubiquitous changes are these:

1. Regularization of tempo and dynamics markings (the latter in smaller type if no source contains the mark).

2. Regularization of slurs, ties and fermatas in parallel parts and parallel passages.

3. Regularization of text elements in "The Four Seasons" (spelling varies considerably from partbook to partbook and also from the presentation in prefatory material to the parts).

4. Elongation of slurs as found in manuscript sources.

5. Correction and extension of basso continuo figuration.

6. Some trills, indicated in smaller type, have been added.

7. Cues referring to texture (*e.g.*, "solo" and "tutti") have been removed.

Changes of pitch, duration and tempo are indicated in the Table of Emendations. Additions and corrections to slurs, ties, fermatas, dynamics and basso continuo figuration are too numerous to be cited.

In his virtuoso passages Vivaldi used two kinds of shorthand. He usually notated chords to represent passages intended for rapid arpeggiation. The pattern of arpeggiation to be used was often written out for one bar only. Sometimes, however, it was not indicated at all but rather left to the discretion of the performer. Arpeggiated passages are fully realized here but the original material is shown in the Table of Emendations. The beginning of a passage that has been so realized is signified in the score by an asterisk (*). Vivaldi sometimes treated articulation in a similar way, giving a one-measure model of slurs or staccatos where the intention was to apply them to several ensuing measures. The application of *simile* articulation is not made except in the case of improving consistency between parts.

Substantially divergent solo episodes for Nos. 7, 9 and 11 are found in manuscript sources. These are reproduced from Vivaldi's autographs in the section called Important Variants. The availability of such material is again signalled at the appropriate point in the main version by an asterisk (*).

TEXT FONTS USED IN "THE FOUR SEASONS"

Three layers of verbal information originating in the printed partbooks are differentiated as follows:

Sonnet texts	*Italics*
Labels derived from sonnets	**Bold**
Performance instructions	Roman

ABBREVIATIONS USED IN THE TABLE OF EMENDATIONS

1. Musical sources

A	Amsterdam print (1725)
D	Dresden manuscript
M	Manchester manuscript
T	Turin manuscript

2. Musical information

INSTRUMENTAL PARTS		RHYTHMIC VALUES		NOTES, RESTS, OCTAVES	
VPr	Violino Principale	w	whole note	A..G	Pitch names
V1	Violino 1	h	half note	g	Grace note
V2	Violino 2	q	quarter note	N	Note (any)
Va	Viola	e	eighth note	R	Rest
Vc	Violoncello	s	sixteenth note	4	Octave ascending from
Bc	Basso continuo	t	thirty-second note		Middle C
		sf	sixty-fourth note	3	Octave ascending to B
		M	measure (any)		below Middle C, etc.
		¦	barline	8^{ve}	Octave

N.B. Elements may be combined, *e.g.* Bq=B quarter note, Rh=half-note rest, G3=the G below Middle C.

General comments may pertain to the work, the movement or the part. Specific comments address a precise location and/or musical object. An asterisk (*) in the Table means that the same change applies in all analogous passages throughout the movement.

TABLE OF EMENDATIONS

WRK	MVMT	PART	BAR^{BEAT}	OBJECT	CONTENT OF SOURCE (A, D, M, OR T)
1	1	Bc	12^4	Ee-Be	A: Eq
1	1	Bc	45	Bs	A: Bt-Bt
1	1	Va	57^2	G♯	A: F♯
1	3	Bc	16^7	B	A: A [♯]
1	3	VPr	17^2	B♯	A: B
1	3	VPr	17^2	A♯	A: A
1	3	V2/Bc	29^1	E♯	A: E/No ♯
1	3	VPr	43	Bq.	A: Bq
1	3	Bc	71	*Tasto solo*	A: *Tasto solo sempre*
2	1	V2/Bc	25	Re Nq	A: Nq Re
2	1	Va	110^1	D	A: C
2	1	VPr	122^2	D♭	M: D
2	1	VPr	122^2	D♭	A: D
2	1	VPr	$154^{2\text{-}3}$	e.	A: s.
2	1	VPr	154^2	g	A: No g
2	1	Bc	$168^{1.5}$	C♯	A: C
2	1	VPr	174	G	A: Measure duplicated as Bar 175
2	2	V2	19^4	D	A: C♯
2	3	V2	13^1	E♭	A: G3
2	3	V2	15^1	G	A: C4
2	3	V2	17^1	B♭	A: E♭4
2	3	V2	17^2	F♯	A: F
2	3	VPr	18^2	F♯	A: F
2	3	V1	19^2	F♯	A: F
2	3	Bc	33	All	M: Written an 8^{ve} lower
2	3	V2	36^1	E♮	A: E [♭]
2	3	VPr	54^1	C♯	A: C
2	3	VPr	51-54	All	A: Notated as follows:

WRK	MVMT	PART	BAR^{BEAT}	OBJECT	CONTENT OF SOURCE (A, D, M, OR T)
2	3	Bc	56^1	E♭	A: E
2	3	Bc	60^2	A♭	A: A
2	3	V2	65^2	A♭	A: A
2	3	V2	66^2	A♭	A: A
2	3	V1	85^1	All C4s	A: A♭3
2	3	VPr	96^1	E♭	A: E
2	3	Bc	96^1	E♭	A: E
2	3	VPr	101^2	F♯	A: F
2	3	V2	102^2	F♯	A: F
2	3	V2	108^2	F♯	A: F

3	1	VPr/V1	$2^{2\text{-}3}$	B♭-A	A: A-B♭
3	1	VPr	35^4	A3	A: C4
3	1	Bc	51^4	E♭	A: E
3	1	VPr	53^2	F♯	A: F
3	1	Bc	59^4	C♮	A: C
3	1	VPr	$60^{3\text{-}4}$	All E♭	A: E
3	1	VPr/V1	62^4	E♮	A: E
3	1	VPr	70^4	C♮	A: C
3	1	Va	81^{4*}	ee	M: q
3	1	VPr/V1	89^3	*Larghetto*	A: No tempo marking
3	1	Bc	80-82	B♮	A: B
3	1	V1/Va/Bc	106	*Allegro assai*	A: *Allegro molto*
3	2	Bc	1	*Il cembalo arpeggio*	M: *Il cembalo arpeggiato ed il Violon e Violoncello piano*
3	3	VPr	39	All	M: Same as Bar 40
3	3	Va	44^1	A	A: B♭
3	3	VPr	60-68	All	A, M: Notated as follows:

3	3	VPr	69	s. chord	A: q. chord
3	3	VPr	78^2	G	A: A
3	3	Bc	82^{3*}	Rs Ns	M: Rs. Nt
3	3	V1/V2/Va	$83*$	Rs Ns	M: Rs. Nt
3	3	VPr	86^3	B♭	A: B
3	3	Bc	96^1	e	A: q
3	3	V2	102	All	A: Measure missing
3	3	VPr	126^1	E♮	A: E
3	3	V1	142	A5	A: F4
4	1	Bc	1	*Violoncello; Basso continuo*	M: *Violoncello, Organo, e Violone*
4	1	Bc	$1^{1\text{-}2*}$	Staccato	M: *tr*
4	1	Bc	$2*$	Staccato	A: No staccato
4	1	VPr	$44*$	Martellato	M: Staccato
4	1	VPr	47^3	D♮	A: D [♭]
4	1	VPr	48^1	D♮	A: D [♭]
4	1	VPr	48-53	All t	A, M: Notated as h double stops
4	1	Va	53^3	D♭	A: D♮
4	1	VPr	54-55	All t	A: Notated as follows:

4   2   The Violoncello obbligato incorporated here demonstrates one way to elaborate the skeleton provided by the continuo. It originates on an unnumbered page, facing p. 10, in the *Basso continuo* partbook of A, suggesting that its publication was an afterthought.

4	2	Bc	1	*Basso continuo*	M: *Violoncello solo, Cembalo [e] Violone*
4	2	V1	1^2	2nd G	M: E♭5
4	2	V1	6^4	2nd A	M: E♭5
4	2	V1	7^2	2nd F	M: D5
4	2	V2	16^2	2nd D	M: B♭4
4	3	VPr/V1,2/Va	30-38	All	M: Staccato
4	3	Bc	36^4	Last t	A: Two sf
4	3	V2/Va	42-47	Martellato	M: Staccato
4	3	VPr	73-79	All Ds	A: Without ♮
4	3	VPr	80^2	A♮	M: A [♭]
4	3	VPr	81^3	D♮	A: D [♭]
4	3	VPr	82^1	D♮	M: D [♭]
4	3	VPr	82^3	A♮	M: A [♭]
4	3	VPr	84^2	D♮	M: D [♭]
4	3	Bc	84-89	Ties	A: No ties
4	3	VPr	85^2	D♮	A: D [♭]
4	3	VPr	86^2	B♮	A: B [♭]
4	3	V2	119^{2-3}	E♭-D♮	A: E♮-D♭
4	3	VPr	120^1	D♮	A: D
4	3	VPr	136^3	D♮	A: D
4	3	V1/V2	138-139	All R	A: Part duplicates VPr
4	3	V1/V2	146-147	All R	A: Part duplicates VPr

5   Notated with two flats in A, D, and M. The first and second violins are doubled by oboes in D, reflecting the greater use of woodwinds in Dresden. Also in D there are two *Organo* and two *Basso* parts for the accompaniment of the outer movements. Pisendel's bowings in D, which are generally longer than those of A, are adopted throughout. Pisendel's *Violino principale* also includes multiple stops on some strongly accented notes and other additional notes. The additional tones are indicated here in cue-size notes. In M the *Violoncello* is marked "tacet" in all *soli*.

5	1	V2	6^3	A♭	A: A
5	1	VPr/V1/V2	14^4	Last D	M: F
5	1	Bc	15^3	C	A: C♭
5	1	VPr	17-26	All	A: Notated as follows:

5	1	VPr	23	All C	M: D
5	1	Va	29-34*	All	M: Duplicates V1/V2
5	1	V1	32^1	D	A: E♭
5	1	VPr	48^{1-2}	All e	A: s
5	1	Bc	48^3	F♮	A: F
5	1	VPr	52^1	All	M: Repeats 51^3

| 5 | 1 | VPr | 58-65 | All | A, D, M: Notated as follows: |

5	1	Va	61¹	D4	M: A♮3
5	1	VPr	66²⁻³	All	A, D: Rq 4 Gs
5	1	V2	66-76	All	A: Part shifted one bar to left, with no R in 66 and all R in 76
5	1	V1	71⁴	B♭	A: B
5	1	Bc	72¹	E♭	A: E
5	1		87	*Allegro*	D, M: *Presto*
5	1		92		M: *Segue subito*
5	2	V2	1³	F	A: G
5	2	V2	4¹	A♭	A: A
5	2	VPr	6¹⁻²	Tie	A: No tie
5	2	VPr	9⁴	E	A: E♭
5	2	V2	13¹	B♭	A: B♮
5	2	VPr	13⁴	G	A, M: B♭
5	2	Va	14³	D4	A, D: G4
5	2		16		M: *Segue subito*
5	3	V1/V2/Va	44	All N	A, D: R
5	3	VPr	49-62		A, D, M: Notated as shown below; the realization combines the rhythmic pattern of the preceding passage with the melodic pattern of the following one [*sopra il basso* = play on the G string]

sopra il basso

5	3	VPr	59	B♮	A, M, D: B [♭]
5	3	VPr	77-105*	Cue notes	D: Double/triple stops (Pisendel's; absent in A, M)
5	3	VPr/V1/V2	91	A♭	A: A
5	3	All	143³	A♭	M: A♮
5	3	VPr	144¹	A	A: B♭
5	3	V1/V2/Va	147-148	All N	A, D: R
5	3	Bc	147	A♮	A, D: A [♭]
5	3	Va	174	B♭3 B♭3	A, D: D4 D4
5	3	Bc	179³	C	A: D
5	3	VPr	198¹	A	A: G
5	3	VPr	199³	F	A: G; M: D
5	3	VPr	206²	G	A: A
5	3	VPr	218*	6 s	A, M: 3 e (E♭-D-C)
5	3	All	221-242	All	M: Omitted; Bar 220 (VPr) = G5q Re
5	3	VPr/Bc	223-242	All	D: Replaced by one bar: qChord C5/E♭4/A♭3 Re (VPr)
5	3	VPr	250	3 F e	M: Fq.
5	3		250-256	Cue notes	A, M: Absent (taken from D)

5	3	Va	259	Dq.	A, D: Dq Re
5	3	VPr	270-275		A, M, D: Notated as shown below; the realization absorbs the rhythmic figuration of Bars 263-269

5	3	V1	289²	B♭3	M: E♭4
5	3	VPr	290¹	Gt	A: Gs
5	3	VPr	290	All	D: E♭s F-E♭t
5	3	All	292	Nq.	A: Nq Re
6	1	Va	15³⁻⁴	Nq Rq	A: Nh
6	1	V1	33¹	G♯	A: G
6	1	Va	34³⁻⁴	e q e	A: q q
6	1	VPr	41	E	A: G
6	1	VPr	42⁴	G♮	A: G [♯]
6	1	VPr	45	All	A: Notated as follows:

6	1	Bc	58⁴	D♯	A: D
6	1	Va	66²	C4	A: B3
6	2	V1/V2	All	All	A: Notated at lower 8ᵛᵉ in bass clef
6	2	V2	1	Clef sign	A: No clef sign
6	2	V1	6⁸	C♯	A: C
6	3	Va	64²	B	A: A
6	3	VPr	76	F♯	A: F
6	3	Bc	76²	B	A: C
6	3	Bc	80²	B	A: C
6	3	Va	98²	G♯	A: G

7	Also printed by John Walsh in *Select Harmony* [London, 1730; reprint, 1732] as No. 1. This republication was based on A.

7	1	VPr	4³	E♮	A: E
7	1	VPr	43-52²	All	A, D: Notated as follows:

7	2	This movement (notated with one flat only in A and T) also occurs in the Concertos in G Major for Recorder, Oboe, Violin, Bassoon and Continuo, RV 101, and for Flute, Strings and Continuo, RV 437 (Op. 10, No. 6). In these works the third movement is a paraphrase of the theme of the second movement.

7	3	VPr	44²	F	A: E
7	3	VPr	65¹	B♮	A: B
7	3	Va	92¹	F	A: E

8   In Vivaldi's autograph (T), the instruments are not specified; unison strings are indicated as "Unis.ⁱ" with initial and terminal notes of *tutti* passages only. Vivaldi's bowings, used here, generally cover more notes than those in A. Vivaldi's *Basso continuo* figures are incorporated here. A suppresses numerous 5/4 figures and often gives 6/5 where 7/5 or 6/4 is correct. This work, which is notated with one flat only in both sources, was also printed by John Walsh in *Select Harmony* [London, 1730; reprint, 1732] as No. 2. This republication was based on A.

8	1	Bc	3³	E♮	A: E [♭]
8	1	VPr	8⁴	E♮	A: E
8	1	VPr/V1/V2	11³	B[♭]	T: ♮ changed to ♭
8	1	VPr/V1/V2	14³	B[♭]	T: B♮
8	1	VPr	26¹⁻²	E♭	T: E
8	1	VPr	30¹⁻²	B♭4q Re	A: 4s (B♭4 D5 C5 B♭4) B♭5e
8	1	VPr/V1/V2	34³	F♮	T: F[♯]
8	1	VPr	37³⁻⁴	8s	A: 4e (F4 A4 C5 F5)
8	1	VPr	39¹⁻²	8s	A: 4e (C5 E♭5 G5 C6)
8	1	VPr/Bc	40⁴	F♮	T: F[♯]
8	1	VPr/V2	85	gF♯	T: No g
8	2	V1	1-7		T: Originally duplicated V2; this was changed to "*Unisoni*"– with V1 matching VPr
8	3	VPr	26¹	e. s	A: e e
8	3	VPr	41-47	All ssss	T: Slurs crossed out
8	3	Bc	48	*Tasto solo*	A: No marking
8	3	VPr	48-75	All	A, T: Notated chordally in h, with some finger position numbers in T, as shown below:

8	3	VPr	65	D♯	A: D
8	3	VPr	104¹	B♮	A: B [♭]
8	3	V1	106-121	All	T: Notated an 8ᵛᵉ lower in bass clef
8	3	V2	106-121	All	T: In unison with V1
8	3	VPr	130	D4 B♭3	A: C4 A3
8	3	Bc	131	*Tasto solo*	A: No marking

| 8 | 3 | VPr | 131-157 | All | A, T: Notated chordally, with some finger position numbers in T (the tied D is missing in Bars 154-158 of A), as shown below: |

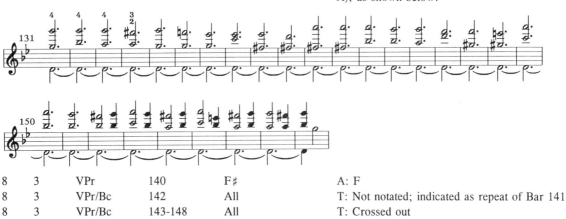

8	3	VPr	140	F♯	A: F
8	3	VPr/Bc	142	All	T: Not notated; indicated as repeat of Bar 141
8	3	VPr/Bc	143-148	All	T: Crossed out

9   The solo instrument in Vivaldi's autograph score (T) is an oboe. The oboe concerto takes the number RV 454, while the violin version is RV 236. To represent this autograph, its slurs (generally shorter than those for violin) are adopted here and its one variant solo is reproduced as Variant 9a.

An independent *Violino primo* is notated (T) only when the part is not in unison with the solo instrument, and the *Violino secondo* and *Viola* are notated only when not in unison with the *Violino primo*. All three parts are sometimes given in the bass clef. The very active *Basso continuo* suggests use of the bassoon. Vivaldi dedicated one of his bassoon concertos, RV 496, to Count Wenceslas of Morzin.

A two-stave continuo is used throughout the second movement in A.

9	1	Va	14	All	A: Notated as a repeat of Bar 13
9	1	Bc	71$^{2\text{-}3}$	4e (A2 B2 C3 D3)	A: A3q D4q
9	1	VPr	73^2	B♮	A: B
9	1	VPr	91-108	All	T: Oboe part shown as Variant 9a
9	1	VPr	99^3	G♯	A: G
9	2	VPr	1, 3	w	A: Tied h h
9	2	VPr	13^3	C♮	A: C
9	3	VPr	26^4	C♮	A: C
9	3	V1	26-32	All	T: Written an 8^{ve} lower in bass clef
9	3	V2/Va	26-32	All	T: Indicated only by unison scoring
9	3	VPr	27^4	B♭	A, T: B
9	3	V1/V2/Va	30$^{1\text{-}2}$	E4..E4	A: G♯3..G♯4
9	3	V1/V2/Va	31$^{1\text{-}2}$	E4..E4	A, T: G♯3..G♯4
9	3	V1/V2/Va	57^3-64^2	All	T: Notated an 8^{ve} lower in bass clef

10   D is largely independent of both A and Vivaldi's autograph (T), particularly in the treatment of the bass instruments: series of detached legatos are substituted here and there for sustained notes. Yet the mock drum roll (e ss q q) of Vivaldi's score is subdued into a tame e e q q pattern in D and A. Inner voices in T are treated much as in No. 9. The title "La Caccia" originates in T. A two-stave continuo is used throughout the second movement in A.

10	1	All		Allegro	D: Allegro assai
10	1	Va/Bc	1^{1}*	e ss	A, D: e e
10	1	V1	5^3	E♭	A: E

10	1	VPr/V1	10³	A♮	A: A
10	1	Va/Bc	19¹-21³*	h.	D: e e e e e (detached legato)
10	1	VPr	32	Martellato	D: No articulation marks
10	1	VPr	31-63		T: Vivaldi gives many finger position numbers (0..3)
10	1	Va/Bc	70-72	h.	D: q e e e
10	1	V2	72³	E♮	A: E
10	1	Bc	83-93	Nh Rq	D: Ne Ne Ne Ne Rq
10	1	V1/V2/Va	131-136	All	T: Notated 8ve lower in bass clef
10	1	Va/Bc	150-152	Tied h. h. h.	D: q e e e e ¦ e e e e e e ¦ e e e q
10	2	VPr	4³	s s e	A: e s s
10	3	Bc	11-13	All	A: = Bar 11 8ve lower + Bars 11-12
10	3	VPr	36, 37	A	D: B♭
10	3	VPr	41, 43, 93, 127¹		T: Finger position numbers "2", "1", "2", "2"
10	3	All	77		T: Seven bars not appearing in other sources are crossed out; the contents resemble Bars 77-82 without jumps into the higher register found in Bars 77, 79 and 81
10	3	All	112	All	D, T: Measure omitted
10	3	V1/V2	130-144	All	T: Notated an 8ve lower in bass clef
10	3	V1	144¹	F4	A: D5
10	3	VPr	147-148	All	T: Vivaldi crossed out the following passage of divisions:

11   The survival of Vivaldi's autograph (T) complicates the task of determining a preferred version of this work. As Ryom has painstakingly noted, the autograph includes parts of at least two versions of the work. The version published by Le Cène (A) corresponds largely to the apparent first version (Version 1), the basis of this edition, but large portions have been crossed out by Vivaldi. The replacement material (Version 2) consists primarily of new solo episodes (shown as Important Variants 11a-d) and creates a shorter movement, since one solo is eliminated. In the third movement, Vivaldi seems to have then modified the ritornello material several times. Variant 11e may have been discarded at an early stage, but the new solo 11f seems to have been followed by a variant of 11e (see the discussion on p. 238).

One additional source for this work is the Manuscript Mus. 5568 in the Wissenschaftliche Allgemeinbibliothek in Schwerin, Germany (indicated below as S). It consists of parts that appear to have been made from the print.

11	1	VPr	28³	E4	A, T: D4
11	1	VPr	31³	E4	A, T: D4
11	1	Bc	43¹	*Tasto solo*	A: No marking
11	1	All	52		T: The next four bars have been crossed out and do not appear in A
11	1	VPr	59³-66²		A: The irregular beaming of T, followed here, differentiates the open E string (shown with a slash across the stem in Vivaldi's autograph) from passages on the stopped A string.
11	1	V1/V2	59³-66²	G♯	A: G (some ♯ missing in T)
11	1	V1/V2	69³-93¹	All	T: Notated 8ve lower in bass clef
11	1	Va	71³	G♯	A: G

| 11 | 1 | All | 84³ | | A: One measure—84³-85² in the example below—is absent in T, all versions, and is omitted here |

Violino principale

Violoncello; Basso continuo

11	1	Bc	86⁴,88⁴	Ee Ce	A: Es Ds Cs Bs
11	1	VPr	122³	G♮	A: G
11	1	V1	122³	C♮	A: C
11	1	VPr	126¹-127²	All	A: Contains instead:

11	1	VPr	132	A4q E5q	A: Eh
11	1	Bc	137¹	D2	A: D3
11	2	V1	4³	*più p*	A: *pia: piano*
11	3	V2	20³	G♯	A: G
11	3	All	28²-31³	All	T: Crossed out; Bar 31 is followed by a 6-bar sketch with double stops in the VPr without Bc or other accompaniment:

11	3	V1/V2/Va	38¹-50³	All N	A: R
11	3	V2	40	G G G	T: A A A [causing parallel fifths with V1 at Bar 41]
11	3	V2	41²-47¹	All N	T: No notation in Vivaldi's autograph, but intended presence of parts suggested by clef signs
11	3	VPr	54³	G♯	A: G
11	3	V2	75¹	G♯	A: G
11	3	All	113-118	All N	A, T: Notated as follows:

11	3	VPr	116¹	G♯	A: G
11	3	All	118+		T: Next bar like Bar 117 but a tone lower; omitted in 1725
11	3	VPr	143¹	A♯	T: A
11	3	VPr	145¹-147³	All	A: Contains instead:

11	3	Va	155²	A	A: A♯
11	3	V2	202³	G♯	A: G
11	3	Va	210³	C♯5	A: A4
11	3	All but Bc	211-213		T: Notated as *col Basso*
11	3		214		T: *Qui si ferma a piacimento*
11	3	All	214		A: Bars 214-216 contain the following VPr (with unison/8ve scoring): D4e D4e G3q A3q ¦ D4e F♯5e G5q E5q ¦ F♯h. This material, absent in S and T, is omitted here, but see the comments under 11e below.

12 A presumed autograph version for oboe (RV 449) is lost. The notes concerning No. 9 give some idea of what difference may have existed between this violin version (RV 178) and that for oboe. A two-stave continuo is used throughout the second movement in A.

12	1	V2	15³	B♭	A: B
12	1	VPr	30³	C♯	A: C
12	1	VPr	56¹	F♯	A: F
12	1	VPr	73¹	B♭	A: B
12	1	Va	83³		A: Superfluous barline removed
12	3	V2	11³	E	A: F
12	3	VPr	17¹	F	A: E
12	3	VPr	17³	F	A: E
12	3	VPr	42³	s s e	A: e s s
12	3	Va	70³	G♯	A: G
12	3	VPr/V1/V2	89³	G♮	A: G
7a	1	VPr	50-51	All N	T: Can be figured as in Bars 42-49 (p. 114)
7a	1	V1/V2	54¹-60³	All N	T: Derived from VPr
7a	1	V1/V2	69³-77	All N	T: Derived from VPr
11b	1	V2	125-129	All N	T: Derived from V1 ["*Et supra*"]
11c	3	VPr	47-50	All N	T: Notated an 8ᵛᵉ lower

11e has its own variant version, notated on one staff only:

| 11e | 3 | VPr/V1/V2 | 177 | D4 | T: D5 |
| 11e | 3 | Va | 177 | D3 | T: A4 |

11f   3   The variant ritornello shown under 11e appears to have been intended to follow the solo 11f (Version 3). However, 11f may have been introduced by a transitional passage of 5 bars, based on this sketch in the tenor clef:

This passage ends with the note "*Qui si ferma a piacimento poi segue*" ("Conclude as you please; then continue"). Ryom believes that the inscription originally said " . . . *poi segue cadenza.*" Variant 11f, a cadenza of sorts, could easily be initiated at Bar 5 of the transitional passage and followed by the variant of 11e shown above. The transitional passage, however, does not enhance the movement musically. A direct transition at Bar 171 to 11f and then to either 11e or its variant above (Version 4) makes more sense.

The rationale for supposing that 11f is excluded from Version 2 is that Vivaldi computed the total length of the revised third movement to be 163 bars.

| 11f | 3 | V2 | 180-208 | All | T: Indicated only as "*Et supra*" |

END OF EDITION